Writing Smarter not harder

The Workbook Way

A proven approach to increasing output and sales through "pre-writing" instead of rewriting.

Colleen L. Reece

Colleen L. Reece

Kaleidoscope Press

Edited by Penny Lent

Kaleidoscope Press
2507 94th Ave. E.
Puyallup, WA 98371-2203
206.848.1118

Toll Free Orders
1-800-977-READ [code] MORE
1-800-977-7323 [code] 6673
(checks—charge cards—purchase orders accepted)

Kaleidoscope Press offers other books, including a series for writers in K-college:

> **Young Writer's Market Manual**, $7.95, ISBN 1-885371-02-0
> **Young Writer's Contest Manual**, $7.95, ISBN 1-885371-05-5
> **Young Writer's Manuscript Manual**, $7.95, ISBN 1-885371-01-2

─────────

Meeker Mansion Mysteries, $5.95, ISBN 1-885371-03-9, Historical fiction, 22 shorts
Dream Like Ezra, $2.95, ISBN 1-885371-04-7, line-art historical picture book, Bird
Clown Ministry Organizer, $15.99, ISBN 1-885371-06-3, How-to & promotion, Amos

─────────

Exploring the Beach Peninsula, Sights/History, ISBN 1-885371-10-1, WA, Etchison,
Interactive Parties & Games for All Ages, ISBN 1-885371-08-X, Rabe & Schneider
Clowning for Beginners, ISBN 1-885371-07-1, Basics, Chuck & Sheila Amos

Printed in the United States of America

International Standard Book Number 1-885371-13-6
Library of Congress Catalog Card Number 95-77207

A 30% discount is given to writing teachers who order a minimum of 10 workbooks.
They also receive a FREE copy of the "Teacher's Manual" designed for this book.

TABLE OF CONTENTS

INTRODUCTION

Who needs The Workbook Way (TWW)?

I do—

and I am a full-time author with 93 published or accepted books and over 1200 story and article sales in the past 20 years—thanks to TWW's unique and innovative "pre-writing to help eliminate re-writing" system.

You do—if you have ever said:

- "I have three children under three. How can I write anything between diaper changes and 'I-wanna-drinka-water' demands?"

- "Writing is my favorite subject at school. I'd like to be an author."

- "I am faithfully writing, even selling. How can I increase sales?"

- "I have great beginnings and endings but go blah in the middle."

- "I'm a single parent with two jobs. I need the basics. Help!"

- "Will I have to compromise my standards in order to sell?"

- "It takes me so long to complete a manuscript I'm sick of it before I finish—and I usually don't. I need to write faster yet keep quality."

- "Work and commuting leave me too brain-dead to be creative."

- "I know I can write. I need a fire built under me to get me motivated."

- "How can I determine if I have it in me to become an author?"

- "I have drawers filled with manuscripts but am afraid to submit them."

- "Do you have a shot in the arm to help me overcome discouragement?"

What good is it to study TWW? Why not just write?

What good is it to study medical texts? Why not just hang out your shingle and wait for the White House to call, asking you to do emergency surgery on the President? Workbooks cannot replace actual writing any more than textbooks replace surgical practice. They do provide guidelines and save you from making mistakes as deadly to your writing career as a false move in the operating room is to the unfortunate patient.

When can TWW be used?

On coffee breaks, lunch breaks, the middle of sleepless nights, on the way to work in carpool or bus. TWW's format fits your busy schedule and provides a portable writing course. The dozens of thought-provoking questions don't have to (and won't) be answered all at once. After you've read them, however, your subconscious can toss them around while you complete other tasks. When you finally have writing time, **you'll have a game plan—a head start** on your manuscript that allows you to get directly into the actual writing.

Where can TWW be used?

On the job, while waiting for that long distance call to a contact who just stepped out for what turns out to be many more minutes than the *one* minute the receptionist promised. During those interminable waits to see a doctor, dentist or client. In airport terminals. Your **portable writing course**, in workbook form, fits neatly into a briefcase or shopping bag and is there when you need it.

Why the Workbook Way?

TWW is certainly not the only good way to write. But it is **a proven, effective** way. It works by requiring writers to lay a solid foundation before attempting to build. Only the intrepid few begin to construct a house without blueprints. Why should writing be different? I am occasionally asked, "Once you've done all that planning, where's the creativity, the joy in writing? Doesn't TWW destroy originality and personal style? Isn't it just write-by-number?"

Not at all. **Once I know where I'm going and how to get there**, I can enjoy the scenery along the way. My mind is free of clutter and ready to weigh all the fresh and wonderful insights that spring from the solid foundation I've created.

In fiction, I can also more intelligently evaluate and draw a fine line between listening to my characters and allowing them to run off on interesting side trips. I know my destination; they do not. It is my job to stay in control by using only those factors that move every sentence of my story closer to the satisfying conclusion.

Blank paper and computer screens can be terrifying. It's a whole lot easier to fill out a workbook page than to tackle a project head-on. I have never used an agent, which means I need the best possible way to operate successfully. I use the same step-by-step approach offered in TWW with all my articles, stories and books. I know once I have done my required "homework" I can complete quality, salable manuscripts.

How can TWW be used most successfully?

By following the suggestions and studying material in the order presented. This system has taken me 15 years to perfect. The temptation is always there to begin writing when a great idea comes. *It's fine to jot it down* but unless the complete manuscript is rushing at you with the speed of light, don't begin even the first draft until TWW asks you to do so. (See <u>Before or After</u>, Part I.) The waiting is worth it. I walked off a good government job with no guarantee I could make it except determination and the belief I had a God-given talent that needed to be used. TWW "pre-writing" cut my rewriting so much I had over 1,000,000 words in print after my first five years of free lancing. So:

- **study every example**--all are from published work--and the analyses.
- **evaluate the stories**, article and book proposal to see why they sold.
- **complete every assignment** pertinent to your current writing project.
- **take time to digest TWW**. Rushing through won't make you an expert.

TWW doesn't promise instant success or fame, just an easier and more effective way to write.

Colleen L. Reece

Persistent 11-year-old Wins Bike

(Colleen Reece started her writing career
with letters to a radio program)

Darrington, Wash.
June 3, 1947

Dear Free for All,

I've heard of the "Gang" as you call them & if they can't guess this, something is wrong. Because, it's easy as pie.

Most of the children around here have bicycles, but I don't have. Daddy goes up every day to fall timber (as we live in the heart of the timber country) and by the time he gets home, the store is closed. But if I had a bicycle, I could go to town & bring things home in the day-time. Although there are lots of trees around here, money doesn't grow on trees & neither do bicycles.

I've written before & so, Free For All, if you don't send me a bicycle pronto, I'm going to spend more money in postage writing to you than the bicycle costs.

If I won it, I would be the happiest girl in the Universe. There is one chance in a million & I'm taking it.

I wrote in on a quiz once & I won some money so I'm signing myself
The Lucky Girl,
Colleen Reece

PART l: "Pre-Write"—not Rewrite

FIRST IMPRESSIONS

What kind of impression would you make wearing a pizza-stained shirt to an interview? Some writers—and not just beginners—send the equivalent of pizza stains to editors. When you approach magazines and book companies, you are competing with thousands of other professional writers and me. This need not stop you from submitting. You have things to offer we don't. It does mean you must know and observe the rules. *Ignorance is no excuse. You must submit your work in a professional manner.*

I used to have the formatting examples in the back of TWW. I moved them to the front so students would (a) know immediately what the market expects; (b) avoid having to break bad formatting habits later.

Proper submissions don't all sell on the first try. Some of them never sell. What they do is impress editors with the fact you're a serious writer who cares enough about your work to send it in professionally.

Even companies that ask for material on computer disk still want hard (printed) copy. When editors request disk submission, ask for their specific guidelines; some want certain margins, no titles on any page but the first, etc. Some need certain type styles. Most want you to let the machine wrap the text and only hit the Return/Enter key at the end of a paragraph, not at the end of the line. One of my publishers asks for single space in place of double, no paragraph indents, centering, boldface, and italics. Another wants 1" margins (in place of the standard 1-½") on top/bottom/sides plus *italics* rather than underlined words. The key is to know and furnish what the editor wants.

> Companies also need to be told
> —make and model of your computer
> —name and version of your word processing program

The following examples show how to format your manuscript acceptably.

MANUSCRIPT FORMATS
page 1

```
name                 ©199-by (name)
address              word count
city, state, zip     rights offered
phone
soc. sec. #


        THE WORKBOOK WAY

   Welcome to TWW. I hope you

   find this writing method ...
```

Other pages: number consecutively throughout (not by chapter)

```
Reece, TWW                        2


   as useful as I do. It can help  you

   avoid writing pitfalls.

        The Workbook Way isn't the only

   way to write salably.  It is ....
```

Books, chapters/chapter titles, pen name (if used)

```
   same as above
   (use real name here)


        VOICES IN THE DESERT

                by
             Gary Dale


           Chapter 1
         "Long Trail Home"

   Jim Sutherland reined in his winded

   horse at the top of the rise.
```

Always enclose SASE (self-addressed, stamped envelope) or SAS postcard

ENVELOPES

```
Name                              STAMP
Address
City, state, zip

(Special info.*)

            J. JONES  EDITOR **
            ANY PUBLISHING CO
            6 FOREVER ST
            ANYWHERE WA 98000
```

** Editor's name in all caps, no punctuation

Use business envelopes (#10) for 1-5 page manuscripts; large manila for longer; Post Office Priority Mail envelopes for books.

**Put notes to editor after return address: *Requested manuscript (if it was); Holiday; Dated; Request for Guidelines; Seasonal; Follow-up; etc.*

COVER SHEET

Cover sheets are normally used only with book length manuscripts to save retyping the first page. Some magazines ask that you do **not** send a cover sheet. Check your marketing guide or magazine guidelines if in doubt. (*Companies can't pay without SSN.)

THE WORKBOOK WAY

by
Colleen L. Reece
street address
city, state, zip
phone
Social Security # *

FOLLOW-UP LETTER, Example

May 10, 1995

T. Jones, Editor
Sun Publishing Company
62 Ocean View Drive
Somewhere, CA 90000

Dear Mr. Jones,

I appreciate your consideration of "Help for Tomorrow" submitted March 4, 1995. May I please have a progress report? Thank you for your response.

Sincerely,

Enclosure: SASE

_____Still considering "Hope." We expect a decision about_____
_____Manuscript has been accepted. Payment: _____enclosed _____follows
_____on publication.
_____Sorry, not for us. Comments, if any_____
_____
_____

Signed_____Date_____for Sun Publishing

BEFORE OR AFTER?

How can an author write 2-8 books a year plus short stories, articles and children's stories, yet not sacrifice quality? *I practice "pre-writing," the thrust of TWW, and eliminate most of the rewriting.* As mentioned in the Introduction, this clears my mind of preparation clutter and frees creativity.

Charts and outlines may be used in two ways:

Before the fact

I fill in charts before starting a manuscript. Like a builder who lays a solid foundation before erecting a house, I know the structure will be a lot stronger because of the undergirding. The charting method offers a solution to the common problem of "middle sag" (having a great beginning and ending then seeing the story go *blah* in the middle). It's also a standard by which to examine new ideas that come during writing.

Measuring article anecdotes or something the characters stand up and want to do against the overall plan, prevents getting sidetracked and losing manuscript focus.

**Warning: never let characters run away with your story.
Listen to their demands but stay in control.
You know the whole picture. They don't.**

After the fact

What about the times when a certain idea clamors to be written? This is a wonderful and exciting experience. Run, don't walk, to get it on paper or into your computer. Write the first draft—even a novel, if you wish—at white heat. Get down everything whirling around in your brain.

But **before you even consider revising or sending work into the marketplace,** complete the outlines and character charts, etc. Answering the tough questions will enrich your work, add depth to your characters and bring up points you may have overlooked. TWW helps you create a more polished, salable manuscript.

Don't let the competition frighten you. Editors continually look for new, fresh writing. There is always room at the top for those who earn the right to be there, writers who are determined to learn and present themselves and their manuscripts professionally.

WRITING FOR LOVE—OR PROFIT?

Writing for love
—of writing, family, friends

Writing for profit
—or to be read, or heard

—are not really that far apart

The key to productivity, improved writing and self-satisfaction lies in turning out work people—including you—want to read.

The same selectivity you use to pick an incident and turn it into an intriguing story or article for editors/readers, helps you zero in on life experiences your family and friends will most enjoy and hold precious. Market skills such as **strong dialogue, building suspense and showing the good and bad in people** change dull, diary-like memoirs to exciting, enjoyable reading.

Tips for presenting the past for both love and profit:

1. **Stay people-oriented.** Places, events, things are interesting but people like people and their doings. Life stories are always more interesting than history. Share on-the-scene events through dialogue so readers feel they are there, rather than being told after-the-fact through "I remember."
2. **Play down the gloom-and-doom.** When presenting tragedies, focus on what good came from them, something learned, etc. **USE HUMOR.** Everyone's better off for a good laugh.
3. **Short and snappy works best.** Just tell it as it is/was. Dwindling magazine space requires much shorter offerings: 500-1500 is a good range and a neat length for family reading.
4. **KISS--Keep It Simple Student.**
5. **Re-live the thrills**. Before writing a treasured experience, take time to remember every detail, every emotion. Then convey those feelings and happenings to readers in a warm, easy manner.
6. **Make sure you have TAKEAWAY.** Some of our most special memories are dear just to us and our families. To sell, nostalgia must offer something readers can *take away* and apply to their own lives.
7. **Most of all, WRITE FOR YOURSELF.** Laugh and cry a little, visit old friends in memory, give thanks you are alive, with unique stories to share. *No one else has your heritage. You can leave a lasting legacy.* The world will be a better place because you lived, learned and passed it on.

"MINI-RESEARCH" STORIES/ARTICLES/IDEAS

Your own life is your richest gold mine for ideas. Making lists of possibilities can help sort pure gold experiences from pyrite (fool's gold). Add your own categories to the following suggestions.

FIRST
day of school
clothes I picked out
money I earned
date/kiss/crush
teacher
big disappointment
away from home
child/grandchild
big success
vacation
memory
flowers

HOLIDAYS
Christmas/Easter
Halloween/4th July
Thanksgiving, etc.
when school unex-
pectedly closed
surprise event with
Dad/Mom, etc.

SURVIVAL
fears, real/imaginary
physical danger
loss of friends or
loved ones
financial loss
caring neighbors
kind strangers
hanging on

RIDICULOUS
bad embarrassment
laughing at self
foot in mouth

FAITH
church/youth camp
divine intervention
something to cling to

CHANGE
transportation
lifestyle
morals/manners
house designs
attitudes

BEST/WORST
friend(s)/enemies
job(s)
times
days
happenings

LAST
day on job
night in old home
day before leaving
for college/military
child to Kindergarten
family reunion
class reunion

GREATEST
need
hope
joy
satisfaction
honor
answered prayer
dream
sacrifice
blessing
single greatest event
 of life

SPECIAL PEOPLE
teachers
parents
children
family members
friends
boy/girlfriend(s)
husband/wife
ministers
strangers

UNUSUAL
events
people
places

HAPPIEST
day/week/year
moment

ARTICLES...............VERSUS.......SHORT STORIES

⇒ **are easier to sell**
⇒ **present facts**
⇒ **sell best at 500-2000 words**
⇒ **make every word count**
⇒ **need revising/polishing**

Some categories:

How to (do almost anything)
Personal experience
Personal opinion
Sharing
Art of living
Inspirational
Humorous
Religious
Advice (no preaching, please)
Interviews

Some ways to write an article:

Exactly as it happened
Real happenings, names changed
Direct approach: "did you know?"
Just the facts/statistics
Explanation with examples
Let me share...
Hard-hitting/expose' (needs
 solid information to back up)

Articles may be written in:

First person: "I learned..."
Third person: "He learned..."
 or "Jane learned..." etc.
Second person: "Do you
 know how to...?"

⇒ **are most salable if genre**
 (category) such as mystery,
 religious, teen, men's, etc.
⇒ **sell best at 500-2000 words**
⇒ **require revising/polishing**

Some categories:

Adventure/Mystery
Confession
Contemporary/Mainstream
Experimental
Fantasy/Science Fiction
Literary
Juvenile/Teen/YA
Men's
Religious/Inspirational
Women's

Some ways to write a story:

First person: gives the advantage of
being inside a character; disadvan-
tage: writer is limited to only what
character sees, suspects, hears, etc.

Third person: emotion perhaps not so
easily portrayed but a little more
freedom from first person constraint.

Simple past tense is usually best.
"Karen sat at the window."
Present tense: good for certain on-
the-spot reporting type writing.
"Karen sits at the window."

STARTER CHART, example

1. **List something from newspaper/radio/TV that stirred deep emotion in you.** The increasing amount of break-ins even in "safe" neighborhoods.

2. **An event from your past that can be expanded.** Being a lonely child and creating an imaginary playmate.

3. **Someone you know/knew who impressed you tremendously and why.** A retired cowhand Mom and I met in Wyoming. He had a fantastic story.

4. **A personal experience that changed your life and how.** Being born and raised in a small Washington logging town during hard times.

5. **A strong opinion you can back up with facts.** Self-confidence and self-esteem needs to be built.

6. **The solution to a problem you recently solved.** Couldn't keep up with demand for books, so I bought a computer! ♥

7. **A place visited that impressed you favorably or unfavorably.** American Southwest--Arizona, Utah, Colorado, etc.

8. **A day you would/wouldn't want to relive and why.** The first time I held a Colleen L. Reece book in my hands. [Note: I have relived it many times and always get the same wonderful feeling, "Is this really mine?"]

9. **A long held dream that probably won't come true.** Ride a dog sled in Canada or Alaska.

10. **Something you do well enough to teach another.** Writing.

11. **Character traits you admire:** loyalty, honesty, courtesy, kindness.
    Traits you despise: sneakiness, bigotry, snobbery.
    These traits bring heroes and villains alive.

12. **A decision you'd like to change.** Believing for too long that becoming an author was an impossible dream.

STARTER CHART

1. List something from newspaper/radio/TV that stirred deep emotion in you._____

_____

2. An event from your past that can be expanded. _____

_____

3. Someone you know/knew who impressed you tremendously and why.

_____

4. A personal experience that changed your life and how. _____

_____

5. A strong opinion you can back up with facts._____

_____

6. The solution to a problem you recently solved._____

_____

7. A place visited that impressed you favorably/unfavorably._____

_____

8. A day you would/wouldn't want to relive and why._____

_____

9. A long held dream that probably won't come true. _____

_____

10. Something you do well enough to teach another. _____

_____

11. Character traits you admire: _____

Traits you despise _____

12. A decision you'd like to change. _____

_____

AFTER THE IDEA--What?

You have your idea—in fact, a bunch of them. Now what? Don't begin writing unless everything's coming like water over Niagara Falls. Ask yourself:
- **. which interests me most**
- **. which is most timely, or dated**
- **. which will take the smallest chunk of time from my hectic life**

Now decide what to do with it. If it's a true experience that entertains, informs or inspires, _an article_ may be the best and most salable way to go. Or a _short story_ based on what happened with names/places, etc. changed. Or a _first person true story_. If your idea is long and complex, filled with possibilities for expansion, perhaps a _book_ is needed. If it's something you know well and have new/fresh information not generally known, a _how to article_ or _nonfiction book_ may result.

What did I do with my Starter Chart?

1. Irritation at invasion of privacy led to an article, "Remember When No One Locked Up?" Sold to _Catholic Digest_ and other magazines.*
2. Nostalgic story "Mary, Come Back" sold several times then became a chapter in a children's serial.
3. The old cowboy inspired, _COMRADES OF THE TRAIL_, family-oriented adventure book for "kids of all ages."
4. Basis for many articles/stories/books, including _A TORCH FOR TRINITY, CANDLESHINE, CROWS'-NESTS AND MIRRORS._
5. Teen article "Believing in You" sold several times.
7. Setting for many books: Western Trails Quartet: _SILENCE IN THE SAGE; WHISPERS IN THE WILDERNESS; MUSIC IN THE MOUN-TAINS; CAPTIVES OF THE CANYON._
9. Inspired research that led to _ANGEL OF THE NORTH_ and _FLOWER OF THE NORTH._

* Once you've sold a story/article, you may be able to sell reprint rights after it is printed, _depending on what rights you sold to a magazine._ (More information in PART 3, Knowing Your Rights.) Each year I make more from reprint short sales than from article/story originals. **Out of print books can also sometimes be resold.**

PART 2: Articles: THE ANATOMY OF AN ARTICLE

The fine line between articles and stories is dwindling. There is still one distinction: ***articles are true, short stories may or may not be***. This doesn't mean you can't and shouldn't use fiction techniques in articles. **Dialogue, description and suspense add a great deal of depth.**

A good beginning contains:
 1. A grabber first sentence that makes reader want to read on.
 2. A sentence or so telling reader what article is about.
 3. Recognition of possible opposition and a firm rebuttal.

In "Tips for Trips with Older Travelers" (complete article, page 23) I **began** with a statement of fact. I added a bit of color, then challenged readers with a question, *"So what's so unusual about the excursion?"* The answer, *"Mom turned 95 a few weeks after we returned"* shows the subject already given in the title. Two more questions dealing with the desire to travel but hesitancy because of someone's age brings up possible opposition. My rebuttal is simple: *"As long as your older traveler is in reasonably good health, forget your worries and go."* A promise follows. *"You'll have the time of your life and so will your passenger."*

Article middles offer a blend of material: quotes and statistics; personal knowledge and experience; case studies showing the experiences of others (often with names changed) and so on. "Tips" uses personal experience and incidents, what worked for us and others, suggestions and quick tips. Underlined subheadings (like the ones here) attract reader attention. So does numbering items. I used both in my article.

Endings vary according to the article. A *"Q"* article is always effective— well-rounded with a quirk. Since I started the article with the day we returned, I chose to end there as well, but with anticipation. *"How well did Mom do? On the day we got home, she asked...."* My quirk? Mom at 94+ looking forward to another good time. If I had written "Tips for Trips with Older Travelers" in a strict tell-the-tale style, I doubt it would have sold once, let alone several times.

Always <u>show</u> what you want readers to learn, don't just <u>tell</u> them.

TREASURE CHEST WRITING, example

Think of your basic idea as a gem--one to be carefully guarded. Put it in the middle of your treasure chest. Other compartments touch and are related to that gem of an idea. Fill them in with anecdote reminders, case studies, facts, etc. you will use in your manuscript.

YE OLDE TREASURE CHEST

OPENING	CASE STUDY	CASE STUDY
Family photograph albums important. Special memories are better.	Grandson associates warm rolls with cold weather and loving Gram.	Janet and Grandmother both had blue Easter dresses and picked dandelions.
TWIST Surprising survey of family times teens remember most.	**FAMILY TIMES TEENS TREASURE** 650 to 800 words	**CASE STUDY** Todd knew Mom or Dad would be there when he played ball.
CASE STUDY Karen's mother came from work, helped her bathe when ill before a visit to doctor.	**CASE STUDY** Foster son cuddling against "Mom" at church and feeling so secure as a child; he cherished memory	**NO MENTION** of nice clothes; kind of house; how much allowance. TIME w/family was #1

TREASURE CHEST WRITING

OLDE TREASURE CHEST

This is a shortcut outlining trick to be used *only when you know your subject extremely well*. Many articles need full outlines in order to be salable.

ARTICLE OUTLINE, example, page 1
Not all questions will be applicable to every article

1. **Proposed title/why/length:** "TIPS FOR TRIPS WITH OLDER TRAVELERS"—describes contents; 1000-1200 words. (Actual: 1145)

2. **Type of article:** How-to/inspirational.

3. **Who it involves:** My mother and I; other travelers.
   When: September 1991
   Where: Western United States
   Why I'm writing it: To encourage others to take older relatives and friends on trips, as long as their health permits.

4. **What happens** (*brief synopsis):* Mom--almost 95--and I took a 3,742 mile driving trip through six western states and had a fantastic time.

5. **Qualifications to write article:** Taking the trip.

6. **Target audience:** Young through senior adults. Older adults can hand it to younger friends/relatives and say, "See? If they can do it, we can, too."

7. **Theme** (*underlying message):* Senior adults need not and should not be deprived of vacations they can enjoy and successfully handle. **Tip: Typing theme and posting next to work area helps you stay focused.**

8. **Reading level:** Junior High (as is most of my writing). It is reported that Reader's Digest observes this level to appeal to its diverse readership.

9. **Style:** Warm and informal. First and second person (me to you); some third person case studies. Use of the different styles is unusual, but necessary to this particular manuscript.

"Tips for Trips with Older Travelers" is printed on page 23. To date, it has sold to *Vibrant Life, Catholic Digest, Evangel, Alive for Sr. Adults, Lifeglow* and *Parent Care,* for a total of $400.+ income. (Multiple sales info. in PART 9.)

ARTICLE OUTLINE, page 1
Not all questions will be applicable to every article

1. **Proposed title/why/length:** _____
   _____

2. **Type of article:** _____
   _____

3. **Who it involves:** _____
   _____
   When: _____
   _____
   Where: _____
   _____
   Why I'm writing it: _____
   _____

4. **What happens (*brief synopsis*):** _____
   _____
   _____
   _____
   _____

5. **Qualifications to write article** _____
   _____

6. **Target audience:** _____

7. **Theme (*underlying message*):** _____

8. **Reading level:** _____

9. **Style:** _____
   _____

You're doing great—keep going →

ARTICLE OUTLINE, example, page 2

10. **Possible opposition:** Some people feel older adults can't travel well.

11. **Rebuttal:** Personal experiences and case studies show this is false.

12. **Opening sentences:** In September 1991, my mother and I returned home to Auburn, WA, from a 3742 mile trip ranging from Idaho's Sawtooth Mountains to the canyonlands of Utah. We hit heat, cloudbursts, thunder, lightning and wind. We came home a little tired but ecstatic. So what's so unusual about the excursion? Mom turned 95 a few weeks after we returned home.

13. **Important points, examples, etc.** (a) Traveling with an older person can be a great experience. (b) Preparation is needed. (c) Suggestions to make trip more successful, ours and others. (d) Quick Tips, such as packing night lights, taking extra medication in case of delays.

14. **Surprise/twist:** N/A (not applicable to this article.)

15. **Climax, for dramatic article:** N/A to "Tips."

16. **Planned closing sentences** (which in all probability will change): Before we even got home, Mom was asking where we'd go next year!

17. **How does it differ from other articles on the same subject?** Check the library's Periodical Indexes to learn what's been done. Many articles about seniors focus on weaknesses, not their strengths.

18. **What can reader <u>take away</u>?** Seniors can thoroughly enjoy a multitude of experiences too often denied by over-protective family or friends.

19. **Markets:** Family, senior, health, general, women's, religious magazines.

20. **Why editors will strongly consider or buy it:** The growing number of senior adults calls for more recognition of their needs, capabilities and interests and offers inspirational examples that seniors can travel.

ARTICLE OUTLINE, page 2

10. Possible opposition: _____

_____

11. Rebuttal: _____

_____

12. Opening sentences: _____

_____

_____

_____

13. Important points, examples, etc. _____

_____

_____

14. Surprise/twist:_____

_____

15. Climax, for dramatic article: _____

_____

16. Planned closing sentences (which in all probability will change*)*

_____

_____

_____

17. How does it differ from other articles on the same subject?_____

_____

18. What can reader <u>take away?</u> _____

_____

19. Markets: _____

20. Why editors will strongly consider or buy it: _____

_____

ANALYSIS OF FILLED-IN ARTICLE OUTLINE

1-4. **Self-explanatory.** Article titles need to give readers a clear idea of what they will get for investing time in reading them. "Tips for Trips with Older Travelers" does just that. The standard 5-W's in questions 2-3 give a concise overview of the major points (who, what, when, where, why).

5. **Qualifications are often not limited to being published.** Although having a full resume is a plus, the fact Mom and I successfully took the trip and sought out others with similar experiences is my best qualification for this particular article.

6. **Taking aim is mandatory.** This means; know who you want to attract. I wanted a wide age range of readers so targeted it accordingly.

7. **A one-sentence theme** kept me on track.

8-9. **You can't go wrong with KISS--Keep it Simple, Student.** A Junior High reading level suits most readers just fine.

10-11. **Don't ignore opposition.** Bring it up then blow it out of the water with your research, anecdotes, personal experiences, etc.

12. **Opening sentences** invite reader along on the trip, get them interested then hit with the unique fact Mom was almost 95 years old.

13. **Knowing important** points provides direction. I knew before beginning the article the general areas I would cover.

14-15. N/A

16. **Planned closing sentences almost always change.** Mine did, but not that much. I simply expanded on the idea.

17. Offering editors something that's merely a rehash earns rejections. I took pains to see that my article was different than those available.

18. <u>**Takeaway is one of the most important factors in your article.**</u> It may be information, inspiration or just a good laugh--but readers need to take away something or they won't read your work again.

19. **Knowing the market is mandatory.** I not only read guidelines but issues of the various magazines where I planned to submit.

20. Self-explanatory. Again, **knowing current lifestyle trends is as vital** to your marketing as knowing magazine word lengths, etc. In this case, the increasing number of older adults who are in reasonably good health gave a plus to my subject.

**Search for new and unusual ways to solve old, familiar problems and you'll have good article subjects.
How-to articles are always popular.**

EFFECTIVE ARTICLE BEGINNINGS

Half the young people today will spend some time in a single-parent family before the age of 18.

Many are children of divorce and need special ministry not now being given by most churches. ("Ministering to Children of Divorce," *Kid's Stuff* + 3 others)

I grew up in an era of clearly designated "man's" work and "woman's" work. Mom and I rarely pumped water or carried wood for our no-electricity-or-running-water farmhouse home. Dad and my brothers cooked and cleaned only if we were sick or away. Later our family dwindled to 80+ year old Mom and me--or "Woe is me," as I mentally labeled my new role. Suddenly a woman whose sole claim to any mechanical ability lay in plugging in and hoping things worked faced the millions of things someone else had always done for her. ("Man's Work, Woman's Work," *Catholic Digest)*

Melissa* lives just down the street. Tom is a quiet sophomore. Karen has a loving family. Mitch is a minister's son. He just broke up with his girlfriend.

What do they have in common? They are all victims of the epidemic sweeping through the teen/YA world: attempted suicide, the so-called "easy way out." ("The Easy Way? No Way!" *event* + 4 others) *names changed

---

From the Old West comes the story of the cowboy who erupted from the bunkhouse, vaulted to his horse's back and rode off in every direction.

Impossible? Not for writers who write richer, not harder. Although many manuscripts must be "single shots," aimed toward specific magazines, multi-purpose manuscripts and their scatter gun approach bag sales and credits. ("Multi-purpose Manuscripts Make Money," *Writer's Nook News)*

Beginnings clearly show subject of articles so reader will know what to expect immediately. *This is especially important in today's busy world.* **If we don't hook readers in the first sentences, we won't interest them at all.**

QUERY INFORMATION (with successful sample)

Always query when marketing book or guidelines says query. If listing says, <u>query or complete manuscript,</u> consider this rule of thumb: *Query if it will cost you money (long distance phone calls, travel) or time--heavy researching, etc.*

Queries need: one single-spaced typed page, 1 ½" margins,; an interesting opening; brief synopsis; overview of author qualifications; planned length; title or working title; mention of available photos; request for permission to submit; checklist; SASE (or SAS postcard with the checklist information-- see next page).

(Your Letterhead)

Date

Barbara Jackson-Hall, Editor
Vibrant Life
55 West Oak Ridge Drive
Hagerstown, MD 21740

Dear Ms. Jackson-Hall:

My mother and I just returned from a 3742 mile trip in 6 western states. We visited parks, relatives and survived unbelievable weather. Mom will be 95 in a few days.

I'm working on a 1000-1200 word article, "Tips for Trips with Older Travelers," designed to encourage readers to involve older people when traveling. It offers a multitude of tips on how to ensure comfort, such as packing night lights and carrying a portable potty. Each includes an example or how the tip adds quality to trips.

May I submit **Tips for Trips with Older Travelers**? I appreciate your response.

Sincerely,

Enclosures: SASE/Resume (if you have writing credits.)

_____Please submit "Tips for Trips with Older Travelers."
_____Overstocked. Try after _____
_____Sorry. Comments, if any_____
_____
_____
Signed_____Date_____ for <u>Vibrant Life_____</u>

SELF-ADDRESSED, STAMPED POSTCARD, example

Re: "Tips for Trips with Older Travelers"

_____Please complete and send.
_____Overstocked. Try after_____
_____Sorry, not for us. Comments, if any

_____

_____

_____

Signed_____Date____for Vib. Life

EIGHT WAYS TO MAKE EDITORS SMILE

1. Offer them what they ask for, not what you think they should run. You can learn this by studying market listings, guidelines and copies of magazines.
2. Be professional, friendly but not familiar. Use editors' first names only after they have established the precedent and called you by your first name.
3. Let them decide what their readers want to see. Rather than: your readers will enjoy... use a low-key, your readers *may* enjoy, find interesting, etc.
4. Show, don't tell. Send a sample chart that speaks for itself instead of telling the editor charts will be included.
5. Do use a checklist with your queries. The one above has won heartfelt thanks from editors who appreciate my desire to make their work easier.
6. Confirm and beat deadlines. When given a writing assignment and a due date, get your work in ahead of time if at all possible. If you cannot make the deadline, let your editor know as far in advance as you can--and it had better be for a reason just short of death.
7. Include social security number and SASE with all queries/manuscripts.
8. Don't argue, just revise. Unless editorial suggestions compromise your standards or destroy your work, rewrite to the magazine's needs.

How to make editors laugh out loud--*and* reject your manuscript.

a. Tell them what a great person and/or writer you are.
b. Tell them you were inspired to write this and not one word is to be changed. *You certainly may have been inspired*, but--a particular editor may not be inspired to publish the work at this time.

ARTICLE COVER LETTER, example

Date   (Your Letterhead)

Barbara Jackson-Hall, Editor
Vibrant Life
55 West Oak Ridge Drive
Hagerstown, MD 21740

Dear Ms. Jackson-Hall:

Thank you for permission to submit, "Tips for Trips with Older Travelers." It is 1145 words.

I appreciate your consideration and look forward to your response.

Sincerely,

Enclosures: Article/SASE

HELPFUL HINTS

1. Don't forget to type "manuscript as requested" under your return address on the envelope . This avoids having it end up in the slush pile (editor's stack of unsolicited manuscripts).

2. Send to the editor who asked to see it. Never send to "Editor" unless market listing directs you to do so. If first name is generic, write "Dear Lee Jones."

3. Have backup places in mind. **Keep track of your manuscripts on cards or a "Submissions Record,"** (sample in Appendix) that keeps you informed about who has what and for how long. When selecting the first magazine or book publisher you wish to approach, write down 6-10 other good markets.

This serves two purposes:
1. You don't have to take time to hunt to see if manuscript is returned, which means you're far more likely to get it back into the mail immediately.
2. It cuts down on disappointment. The next place on the list may just be the one who will love (and buy) my manuscript.

**Goal with returned manuscripts:
In one day, out again the next,
until they sell or I run out of editors
they might interest.**

Tips for Trips with Older Travelers

In September 1991, my mother and I returned home to Auburn, WA from a 3,742 mile trip that ranged from Idaho's Sawtooth Mountains to the canyonlands of Utah. We also traveled through southern Colorado, northern New Mexico and Albuquerque. Our almost-two-week drive took us to national parks and relatives, through heat, cloudbursts, thunder, lightning and wind. We came home a little tired, but ecstatic over our much needed vacation.

So what's so unusual about the excursion? Mom turned 95 a few weeks after we returned.

Do you know an older person who would love to go on a trip but hesitates because of age? Or do you have reservations about starting out with that friend or relative who is also a senior adult? As long as your older traveler is in reasonably good health, forget your worries and go. You'll have the time of your life, and so will your passenger.

From this trip and many others plus conversations with others comes a variety of tips for trips with older travelers.

Think ahead. Consider your itinerary with your companion in mind but don't be afraid to include places you want to see that may be difficult for him or her. When we visited Mesa Verde Natl. Park in Colorado, Mom didn't feel like doing much walking in the 8500 ft. altitude. Solution? We parked in a shady spot and unloaded the folding lawn chair we carry for shopping at our malls. Mom could see the cliff dwellings across the canyon while I hiked. I returned to find friendly travelers clustered around her chatting. Several commented, "What a good idea to bring your own chair. I'm going to do that with my parent."

Consider your companion's interests, too. You may need to allow for a little more time in getting around.

Keep a regular schedule. Most seniors prefer a set routine of on-time meals and a regular bedtime. If you will be in the middle of nowhere at noon, have a picnic lunch or easy snacks: crackers, jelly, fresh fruit. Carry plenty of drinking water. Medications need to be taken consistently.

Avoid the exotic. One night we arrived late at our destination. We tossed and turned all night following a tasty, but too-filling Mexican meal. If you want food your companion normally doesn't eat, have it at lunch.

Eliminate embarrassment factors. A friend's father almost dreaded going on a motor trip because he frequently required a bathroom quickly and some highways may not have rest areas close enough together. Tim quietly packed a portable potty. His father never needed it, but knowing it was there for an extreme situation proved comforting.

Stop to smell the flowers and rest. Stop the car every hour or so at a rest area, service station or even on a side road to simply walk around the car and stretch.

Wear loose clothing. A long-sleeved, loosely woven shirt protects arms from sun that shines into even an air-conditioned car. Suggest that your passenger kick off shoes and/or prop feet on a pillow.

Take a soft pillow to use as a backrest. Car seats get hard after hours of driving.

Seek out peace and quiet. Senior adults can enjoy excitement. They also need rest. Look for off the highway motels to reduce the noise factor from traffic. At least, request a room on the back side and away from the street.

We always carry a small electric fan. Its hum drowns out noise inside and outside the building. If other guests are noisy beyond reason, call the manager. You have a right to a good night's sleep.

Some quick tips.
1. Pack a night light. Waking in unfamiliar, ever-different rooms can lead to groping, stumbling or even a fall on the way to the bathroom.
2. Double check necessary medicine, glasses, etc. before leaving. We always take extra in case of delay in returning.
3. Lighten the load. A good warm sweatshirt can replace sweater and jacket. An umbrella eliminates need for raincoats. Don't skimp on appropriate clothing, however. Older travelers often need extra warmth. Take car blankets.
4. Take a digital clock with large, red numerals.
5. Don't bother with books. You probably won't have time to read them.
6. Start out right. We asked God to protect and guide us. We took a devotional book and Bibles. We began and ended each day with prayer.

How well did Mom do? On the day we got home, she asked, "Where are we going next year, and the next, and...?"

Mom died in Aug. 1992. Our last trip is one of my most special memories.

PART 3: Tools and Terminology

Mandatory for those who write to sell: a good dictionary, thesaurus, style book (*Chicago Manual of Style* or Strunk and White's *The Elements of Style* are widely used). Also, at least one marketing book that will provide you with hundreds/thousands of places to offer your work. Choose the most applicable to what you're writing.

- *Writer's Market,* available in book stores
- *Literary Market Place,* book stores
- *Children's Writer's & Illustrator's Market,* book stores
- *Christian Writers' Market Guide,* Sally Stuart/Harold Shaw Publ.
- *The Guide to Religious and Inspirational Magazines* (profiles of over 500 publications--saves sending for guidelines)
- *Mystery Writer's Market Place/Sourcebook,* book stores
- *Novel & Short Story Writer's Market,* book stores
- *Religious Writers Marketplace,* Abingdon Press/Chr. book stores

For writing fiction, get a **name-the-baby** book with origins and meanings.

There are dozens of good writing books, Christian and secular. Browse libraries and book stores to <u>find the ones that best meet your needs</u>. My all-time favorites are older books (some have been updated/reissued):

- *Beginning Writer's Answer Book,* Kirk Polking.
- *Fiction is Folks & Secrets of Successful Fiction,* Robert Newton Peck
- *How to Write and Sell Your Personal Experiences,* Lois Duncan
- *Writing Short Stories for Young People,* Stanley (good for all ages)

Market listings in *Writer's Digest* and *The Writer* (secular); *The Christian Communicator* (American Christian Writers); *Writers Information Network* newsletter; Elaine Colvin, Director; offer "what's hot/what's not" help.

COMMON WRITING TERMS

Complete lists of terms and rights, etc. are found in marketing book glossaries and help sections. These are the terms I'm most often asked to define or discuss.

Agents are hard to get unless you have some kind of track record.

Assignment: An editor pre-approves a certain manuscript.

By-line: *TOM SAWYER*, by Mark Twain; identifies author.

Contracts: Normally for books only. <u>Never sign a contract until a professional author or literary lawyer has read it.</u>

Copyright: Current copyright law protects work from the time authors create manuscripts for their lifetime + 50 years. Always show copyright notice on first page, i.e., ©1994 by Colleen L. Reece. There is little need to register with the US Copyright Office unless ownership is questioned. Publishers routinely take care of copyright registration for books.

Genre: Category, such as mystery, romance, western, teen/YA, etc.

Kill fee: Paid when for some reason an assigned manuscript isn't used after all--a percentage of the original agreed-on price.

Payment for <u>books</u> will be made with a contract, either a royalty and advance setup, or an outright purchase.

Payment for <u>articles/short stories</u> will be:

1. <u>On acceptance</u> (preferred). Magazine pays when they **accept** work.
2. <u>On publication.</u> You don't get money until your work is printed. Unless you sell to a large magazine for big bucks or can't sell to a place that pays on acceptance, think twice. **Exception:** Some magazines (especially smaller ones) purchase one time (simultaneous) rights. This means you can sell elsewhere while waiting so it's fine to let an editor hold. **See Rights.**
3. <u>Outright purchase.</u> A flat, one-time fee for your manuscript.

Pen Names: Use only to protect yourself or if requested by an editor. I don't care for them, but male readers are often leery of female western writers, so I am <u>Gary Dale</u> for my Christian western novels, such as *Voices in the Desert/Echoes in the Valley*.

Records: You must keep detailed records of writing income and expenses. If you have questions, consult a good tax accountant, lawyer or IRS.

Knowing your RIGHTS

You have total control over the rights you sell. I recommend that you study a more detailed account of what they are/how they work than this overview.

Book Rights will be spelled out in your contract along with subsidiary (movie, foreign translation, etc.) rights.

Story and Article Rights

1. **All rights:** Just that. Magazine or publisher has no obligation to allow you to even quote your own work.
2. **First North American (NA) serial rights:** The right for a periodical or magazine to publish story/article <u>first in NA.</u>
3. **First serial rights.** The right to publish it <u>first</u> in a magazine or periodical <u>anywhere in the world.</u>
4. **First rights.** The right to publish <u>first</u>. This means you can't include an article or story even in a book until it is published by the magazine.
5. **One time (simultaneous) rights.** The right to use your manuscript <u>once only,</u> at their discretion.
6. **Second or reprint rights.** The right to print <u>after</u> it was published elsewhere.
7. **Foreign serial rights.** If you sold only NA serial rights, you may market simultaneously, **except to US/Canada.**
8. **Work-for-hire.** You contract to write something for a flat fee, the same as a neighbor boy hires out to mow the lawn for $10. When work is done, you're paid and they own all rights forever.

Self and subsidy Publishing: This can be risky. Consult with an expert.

Simultaneous Submissions: Fine for <u>short stories and articles</u> that say they accept them--so long as they are to <u>non-competing magazines.</u>
Can create problems with <u>book-length</u> manuscripts. I prefer to go with proposal/sample chapters, as described in PART 7, MARKETING.

Slush pile: Stack of unsolicited (uninvited) manuscripts on editors' desks.

Speculation: The opposite of an assignment. Editors agree to read but not buy.

Tear sheets/clips: photocopies of your published story/article sent at company's request. **Tip:** Don't send poetry clips if querying a science article,
The clip should show your ability to write the type of project you propose.

Unsolicited manuscripts: Sent without editor permission. Some places won't read or return anything they didn't specifically request.

⇒ If you haven't written your first draft of the queried article, do so now.
⇒ If you have, go to PART 8, LEARNING TO EDIT and begin polishing.
⇒ Don't submit until you have completed all of the PART 8 lessons.

PART 4: Short Stories
THE ANATOMY OF A SHORT STORY

Three is Key:
(for Novels, too)

Short stories start with:
—an interesting individual
—an inspiring setting, or
—an intriguing incident

They present 3 c's
—a strong <u>c</u>haracter
—in meaningful <u>c</u>onflict
—resulting in <u>c</u>hange

They contain:
—an appealing beginning
—an attention-holding middle
—a satisfying ending

A good breakdown
—1/3 <u>h</u>ook*
—1/3 <u>h</u>old**
—1/3 <u>h</u>ighlights***

   *__HOOK__ introduces character(s); sets stage; plunges into problem

  **__HOLD__ develops characters; makes situation worse; shows little/no hope

***__HIGHLIGHTS__ presents crisis (**black moment when all seems lost and
     the problem must be faced)**; lead character's choice; conclusion
     showing how character changed because of that choice

Example: A 1500 word story (roughly 6 double spaced, typed pages) would
     have approximately 2 pages/500 words per "H" above. <u>Don't be
     concerned if your story doesn't match exactly</u>. These are
     suggested breakdowns only.

To live, breathe and sell best, short stories should:
♦ **run less than 2500 words**
♦ **not cover too long a time span**
♦ **have one "star"--the lead (viewpoint character)**

Short stories consist of:

♦ <u>dialogue</u> to move plot forward, bridge time gaps and share insight
♦ short, blended in <u>description;</u> strong verbs add color
♦ <u>narration,</u> simple storytelling interspersed with dialogue/description

TREASURE CHEST WRITING, example

Think of your basic idea as a gem—one to be carefully guarded. Put it in the middle of your treasure chest. Other compartments touch and are related to that gem of an idea. Fill them in with important points, obstacles and temporary victories, etc. you will use in your true or fictional short story.

You may also use it for preliminary outlines of book chapters.

YE OLDE TREASURE CHEST

TRUE EXPERIENCE	STARTS WALK	TAKES CONTROL
From Mom's early married life near Darrington, WA	Dusty road, little traffic Pickup truck stops. She thinks it's a neighbor and gets in.	Silently prays. Says in loud voice, "Stop this truck right here!"
OPENING Nice day, hangs out clothes; lives three miles from town	"STRANGER DANGER" as told to Colleen L. Reece by her mother	VICTORY Driver slows; she leaps and runs. He tears off; not seen again. She gives thanks.
DECISION Finishes work, will walk to town and ride home with husband after work.	ALARM Looks into stranger's eyes. Reaches town. He speeds up when she tells him to stop.	845 words printed in. *Evangel.*

TREASURE CHEST WRITING

YE OLDE TREASURE CHEST

This is a shortcut outlining trick to be used only when you know your subject *extremely well*. Many stories need full outlines in order to be salable.

SHORT STORY OUTLINE, example, page 1

1. **Proposed title/why/approx. length:** "Better to Give" shows at times it really is "better to give than to receive," 1500 words (Actual: 1445).

2. **Markets:** Teen/Young Adult, secular and religious.

3. **Lead/important secondary characters:** Jill, 17, neat but human enough to feel embarrassment. Rod Canning, a boy she likes. Larry Stokes, whose problem becomes Jill's.

4. **Theme** (one-sentence underlying message): Sometimes it really is better to give than to receive.

5. **Plot** (brief synopsis): Jill suggests that her class hold an "Awareness Dinner" to learn about the feelings of those who live with physical challenges. At the dinner, she is paired with Larry Stokes, who helps her make it through an impossible, humiliating evening.

6. **Lead character's problem at beginning of story:** Convincing class to try something different for their charity fund-raiser.

7. **How it gets better or worse:** Class accepts idea and Jill's boyfriend is all for it.

8. **Obstacles/temporary victories** (2-3 are good for a short story): Jill must present/defend her idea to the student body. She does it well. At dinner Jill draws Larry Stokes for a partner. She handles it by determining to be a good sport. Jill is crushed when she discovers her assigned role.

9. **Setting and time period:** High school, anywhere; contemporary.

10. **Why are you writing this story?:** To encourage teens to consider the feelings of others. "Blind Date" (magazine changed title) is printed on pages 36-37. It first sold to *Listen* (secular) then a Christian version sold to *event, HiCall, Young and Alive, Between Times* and *Insight* for a total of $375 plus.

SHORT STORY OUTLINE, page 1

1. Proposed title/why/approx. length: _____

_____

2. Markets: _____

3. Lead/important secondary characters: _____

_____

_____

4. Theme: _(one-sentence underlying message)_: _____

_____

5. Plot (_brief synopsis_): _____

_____

_____

_____

_____

6. Lead character's problem at beginning of story: _____

_____

_____

7. How it gets better or worse: _____

_____

8. Obstacles/temporary victories (_2-3 are good for a short story_): _____

_____

_____

_____

9. Setting and time period: _____

10. Why are you writing this story?:

_____

_____

So far, so good—keep going →

SHORT STORY OUTLINE, example, page 2

11. **What qualifies you to write this story:** Basic incident happened to a teen friend of mine; I wove story around it.

12. **How will lead character change during story:** From being concerned with how she looks to genuine concern for someone else.

13. **Opening sentences** *(they nearly always change)*: For as far back as I can remember, Dad and Mom have always told me it's better to give than to receive. Part of the time I even agree with them....

14. **Surprise or twist:** Discovering that embarrassment isn't always negative.

15. **Possible closing sentences** *(which will definitely change)*: What if Larry hadn't been my partner? Maybe I would have taken a whole lot of things for granted that I think about more seriously now.

16. **Clues planted for reader:** We know Jill is compassionate and caring because of her original suggestion. We know she is mature from the fact she is willing to offer a startling suggestion to her class.

17. **Why an editor will buy and readers will remember:** It's timely due to the emphasis being placed on positive things people can do instead of dwelling on what they can't.

18. **What feeling you want to leave with readers:** The feeling we can be blessed when we extend ourselves on the behalf of others.

19. **Does the planned ending fit? Will readers find it acceptable?:** Yes. Jill may be spaghetti stained outside, but inside she is thankful for the traumatic experience because of what she learned.

20. **Is the story believable?:** *(Remember, some real happenings are so bizarre readers won't find them plausible when they're told as fiction.* This story is based on truth and readers do find it believable.

[*Listen* Magazine is used for discussion starters on issues, in public schools.]

SHORT STORY OUTLINE, page 2

11. What qualifies you to write this story:_____
_____

12. How will lead character change during story:_____
_____

13. Opening sentences:_____
_____
_____

14. Surprise or twist: _____

15. Possible closing sentences: _____
_____
_____
_____

16. Clues planted for reader:_____
_____
_____

17. Why an editor will buy and readers will remember: _____
_____
_____

18. What feeling you want to leave with readers:_____
_____

19. Does the planned ending fit? Will readers find it acceptable?:_____
_____

20. Is the story believable?:_____
_____

Note: Before writing your story, complete a character chart on lead character(s) and enough detail on other characters to bring them alive.

ANALYSIS OF FILLED-IN SHORT STORY OUTLINE

1-2. <u>Self-explanatory</u>. I knew this story could either go secular or Christian, depending on its setting. No more than 1500 words is a good length for teen/YA stories.

3. <u>Appealing characters</u> are a must in most stories. They need their problems so readers can relate, but who wants to read about a whiner or spoiled brat? Jill is attractive but not unbelievably beautiful. Rod is understanding and honest enough to admit his doubts. Larry is a winner. He reaches past his own limitations to comfort Jill.

4. <u>Clichés</u> weaken writing but make excellent themes!

5. <u>Story needs to move</u> to hold readers, especially children and teens/YA.

6-7. <u>Getting a date for a special event</u> is no longer enough justification for a story. Today's young people are absorbed in current issues and events.

8. <u>No obstacles, no story.</u> Remember: character, in conflict, resulting in some kind of change due to character's decision.

9-10. <u>Self-explanatory.</u>

11-12. <u>Self-explanatory.</u> Jill's concern for others is evidenced in the beginning and sets a natural climate for her change after a tough experience.

13. <u>I chose first person</u> to invite readers inside Jill and began with an old saying, to which humor is added through Jill's rueful agreement with her parents' advice.

14. <u>A surprise/twist/quirk</u> sets your story apart from other similar ones.

15. <u>Planned ending sentences always change.</u> However, knowing where you want to end up with your story keeps you on track while writing it.

16. <u>Surprises must follow rules.</u> Don't make drastic changes in your characters without planting clues. Christian authors are especially guilty of having characters suddenly change their lifestyle for the better on the spur of the moment. Neither should likable, supposedly decent characters become monsters unless a proper foundation is laid.

17. <u>This comes back to knowing the market.</u> By keeping up on current issues I knew this subject would be well received.

18. <u>Self-explanatory.</u>

19-20. <u>Endings must always be acceptable.</u> A high percentage of readers prefer happy endings. If you must have a sad or tragic ending, make it acceptable. **Example:** A friendly neighborhood storekeeper ruthlessly gunned down will bring protest. If he's killed saving someone else, readers still won't like it, but can accept it for the good it brought.

EFFECTIVE SHORT STORY BEGINNINGS, examples

Your story beginning is crucial. Most editors read only the first page of your story (about 2 paragraphs). If you haven't hooked them, they stop. (More on Multiple Sales in PART 9, PERSEVERANCE PAYS.)

THE LIVING ENCYCLOPEDIA
(humorous early teen)

When Mr. Foster, our ninth grade social studies teacher, announced it would be girl/boy matchups for our next assignment, Bobby Nicholas hollered, "I'll take Jilly." I could have died. Don't get me wrong. Bobby Nicholas isn't a wimp or jerk or creep but his sense of humor is weird. After I got a beautiful tan rabbit for a pet, every time Bobby Nicholas saw me he started singing, "I dream of Jilly with the light brown hare."

You can see I couldn't expect a lot of help with our project, and I needed a good grade to bring up my average. (*Young and Alive*)

WEEKEND DAD

"Will this be all right, sir?" The waitress pointed to a four-person booth in Denny's.

"Fine." The young man shifted his two-year-old daughter from left to right arm, captured his three-year-old son's reluctant hand and went to the booth.

After one sobbing *I-want-Mommy* spell, the arrival of two high chairs and then lunch, an uneasy peace settled on the little group. (*Evangel, Live, Lifeglow*)

I DON'T KNOW YOU *(children)*

"Kristi. Kristi Turner," a man standing next to a car near the school yard called. Kristi turned.

"Your mother wants me to bring you home right away," the man said. "Hurry. Your father's been hurt and is in the hospital."

Kristi took a step toward the car then stopped. "I don't know you."

"It's OK. Do I look like the kind of creep who goes around picking up kids?" The stranger smiled.

He really didn't look creepy, Kristi decided. Yet why would Mom send someone she didn't know--and on a day when Kyle [her twin brother] had gone home with a friend? (*Primary Treasure, R-A-D-A-R*; part of series of "Kyle & Kristi" stories)

THREE GIFTS OF THE WEAVER

Long ago in a faraway country, a woman named Amaris (whom God hath promised) feverishly worked to complete the garment before her. Outside came the muffled cries of a city freeing itself from daily tasks and anticipating the coming holy days. Amaris' work-worn hands flew, racing the dying light from the already setting sun. She must finish before its last rays disappeared... (*Lifeglow*)

BLIND DATE

by Colleen L. Reece

For at least 15 years (that's as far back as I can remember) Dad and Mom have always said, "It's better to give than to receive." Sometimes I've agreed with them, like the Christmas Aunt Alice sent this hideous heirloom vase. I had to write a thank-you note for it--even though I wished I could call the emergency number at Goodwill.

Last week I found out it's not only better to give than receive; sometimes it's a whole lot easier.

After the holidays our senior class got desperate for money. I love going to a small high school but when there are only about 40 in your class, raising money for all the senior events can be hard. We'd already gone the usual route: car wash, bake sales, a slave auction. I ended up at Mrs. Scrooge's home and washed a million windows. She gave me $5.00.

Maybe it was the memory of my dead-looking fingers from all the cleaner that made me suggest what I did.

One of our school traditions is for each graduating class to sponsor an activity and give the proceeds to charity. We'd chosen a group that helps disabled persons train for jobs.

"Why don't we give something in addition to money?" I asked. "What do we really know about some of the problems people have? Let's sponsor an 'Awareness Dinner.' Each person will be assigned a challenge: a broken leg, hearing disability and so on. We can work in pairs to overcome the difficulties."

After all the buzzing, the kids agreed. Our faculty adviser promised the Home Ec crew would prepare the meal. We'd invite the juniors and sophomores and only charge $3.00.

Our principal beamed. "What a great idea! Jill, be ready to answer questions at the student body meeting when I announce it."

No problem. Still, I took extra time with my appearance the day of the assembly. The way Rod Canning watched me when I climbed into his restored Mustang told me it was worth it.

"New sweater?"

"Uh huh." Glad Rod had noticed, I still sighed. The yellow wool did great things for my dark hair and eyes but even on sale it had nearly bankrupted me. "This awareness thing is one of the best projects our school has done."

He concentrated on his driving. "Too often we never stop to think how good we have it. Wonder how we'll feel?" He grinned. "One thing, it's only temporary."

I shivered in spite of the warmth of the car. Rod wasn't the only one worrying about role playing.

Tickets to the Awareness Dinner sold like front row basketball seats. I couldn't walk three steps from my locker without someone calling, "Hey, Jill, good old Sutherland High's going to make history with this."

On the night of the dinner, most of the juniors and sophs plus all the seniors crowded into the cafeteria. After Rod welcomed us I said, "Number off in twos. All the ones write their names on the papers Rod gives you and the twos draw." I reached in the fishbowl. "See? It's painless." Everyone roared. Was I glad for the confusion when I saw I had drawn _Larry Stokes!_ What strange fate had given me Larry? He's the only physically disabled student in our school. At five, a speeding car put him in a wheelchair. He's a sophomore and gets totally frustrated when he can't get the words out to say what he's thinking.

Well, this was an awareness dinner. As the folks said, it was better to give than to receive. I'd do all I could to make Larry have fun. He must have felt confident or he wouldn't have come.

Finding partners had been confusing. Drawing for challenges was chaos. I helped bandage heads, issue crutches, stuff ears with cotton and arrange slings. I even laughed when I gave Larry his "broken arm." His smile took away some of my dread. Then I drew the last slip. It read:

"You are blind"

I just stared until Larry said, "What--are--you?"

"Blind." I dropped down in front of his wheelchair so he could adjust the blindfold, glad he couldn't see my face. How could we manage? A rush of hatred for the darkness left me trembling. I wanted to tear off the cloth. My hand went up but Larry said, "It's--all--right--Jill. I'll--help--you."

I stumbled to my feet. Everyone in the room was probably looking at me and pitying me. If the whole ghastly idea hadn't been mine, I'd have split.

I steered Larry into the food line at his directions, knowing things couldn't get worse. They did. Dinner was spaghetti.

Rage filled me. How could they be so insensitive? I felt sweat start under my blouse. How could I help Larry or feed myself when I couldn't <u>see</u>?

The nightmare went on. I knew my white blouse and jeans were streaked with spaghetti sauce. Only Larrry's supporting voice saved me. "You--can--do--it--Jill. Move--your--fork--to--the--right. Wind--the--spaghetti."

An eternity later Rod announced dessert and said we could discard our role playing. I yanked off my blindfold. When I saw the utter ruin I'd made of Larry and myself, I mumbled, "Excuse me" and ran.

Before I got to the door of the girls' room, a strange feeling hit me but I managed to hold back tears until I was alone in a stall. It wasn't the humiliation that hurt me. It was learning how those who lived with differences felt, trying to deal with careless things others do daily.

I had felt stared at, angry and ready to strike out against the world. Larry had been patient but I'd found it hard to accept help even when I needed it so badly.

"Its not for keeps," Rod had said. Shame and relief weakened my knees and made me choke. I washed my hands and face, trying to get my emotions under control. My jeans and blouse would have to wait. I slipped back into the cafeteria. All the kids--except Larry--had put away the slings, bandages, crutches and blindfolds. He sat in his wheelchair, waiting.

I hurried to him, undid his sling and took a deep breath. "You'll never know how glad I am you were my partner." I bit my lip. Hard. "Thanks."

"I understand--Jill." His deep blue gaze looked into me.

Somehow I knew he did.

PART 5: Characters

Plot and setting are important—but **characters make your story or novel salable and memorable.** This extensive chart is designed to help you know your characters inside and out so you can select the right one for each job.

CHARACTER JOB APPLICATION, example, page 1

Part I: Physical Data

1. **Name/why chosen:** ANDY CULLEN. Andrew means strong, manly. This fits his personality.

2. **Age:** 19 when story opens. **Note:** When writing for juveniles/YA, make lead characters the upper age. Example: stories for 8-12 need 11-12 year old hero/heroine or only the 8-10 year olds will read the story.

3. **Height/weight/general build:** 5'9", 160 lbs., lean and sinewy.

4. **Eyes:** <u>Color:</u> brown. <u>Shade:</u> sparkly, with little gold motes. <u>Shape:</u> round. Close set, wide set, protruding, deep set: wide set. <u>Size of eyes:</u> large. <u>Wear glasses:</u> no. <u>Lashes:</u> thick, stubby, pale, sparse: thick and stubby. <u>Brows:</u> thick, sparse, straight, curving: thick and straight. Sentence that describes eyes/eyebrows/lashes: Mischief motes danced in brown eyes that looked the world square in the face.

5. **Ears:** <u>Size/shape:</u> normal. Sentence about ears: Andy's ears looked quite ordinary, but could hear the slightest rustle in a bush.

6. **Nose:** <u>Size/shape:</u> generous, a bit tilted. <u>Mustache</u> (if so, what kind; bristling, moth-eaten, well trimmed). No mustache. Sentence about nose: Andy kept his nose out of other folks' business and let it grow.

7. **Hair:** <u>Color:</u> ripe corn. <u>Springy, oily, straight, curly, wavy:</u> springy. <u>Thin, thick, long, short, receding hairline. Sideburns (style), Beard.</u> Thick and shocky looking but short. No sideburns or beard. Sentence about hair: Andy's tossing mane resembled the manes of the wild horses he pursued at full gallop.

CHARACTER JOB APPLICATION, page 1

Note: Don't expect to sit down and complete a character job application in one sitting. If you do, it will be surprising. Some questions in the latter part of the chart are super-tough, designed to make you know your character through and through.

(One student who did a chart on her husband found it took weeks to complete and they had been married 40-plus years!)

Part I: Physical Data, (add your own description as needed)

1. Name/why chosen:_____

_____

2. Age: _____

3. Height/weight/general build: _____

4. Eyes: Color: _____ Shade: _____Shape:_____
Close set, wide set, protruding, deep set: _____ Size of eyes:_____
Wear glasses: _____ **Lashes:** thick, stubby, pale, sparse:_____
Brows: thick, sparse, straight, curving: _____ Sentence
that describes eyes/eyebrows/lashes:_____

_____

5. Ears: Size/shape: <u>normal.</u> Sentence about ears:_____

_____

6. Nose: Size/shape: _____ Mustache (if so, what kind;
_____ Sentence about nose: _____

_____

7. Hair: Color: _____Springy, oily, straight, curly, wavy:_____
Thin, thick, long, short, receding hairline, sideburns (style), beard.
_____Sentence about hair:_____

_____

CHARACTER JOB APPLICATION, example, page 2

8. **Skin:** <u>Color, texture, soft, weather-beaten, smooth, pocked, wrinkled:</u> tanned, smooth, wrinkled around the eyes. Sentence about skin: Clear, tanned skin spoke of Andy's outdoor life. So did the wrinkles around his eyes earned by endlessly watching the changeable Utah canyonlands that lured him on in search of Sheik.

9. **Mouth:** <u>Size, shape, thin/full lips, cupid's bow, pale, lipsticked, crooked, cracked or smooth lips, usual expression:</u> Wide, generous, thin-lipped but tilted into happy grin most of the time. **Teeth:** <u>Even, crooked, color, any missing</u>: Strong, even, white. Sentence about mouth/teeth: His irrepressible smile could anger an enemy and delight a friend.

10. **Shape of face:** <u>Round, oval, heart-shaped, square, etc.:</u> oval. Sentence about face: A good face, open, honest, demanding the same of others.

11. **Neck:** <u>Scrawny, wrinkled, graceful, smooth, strong:</u> Smooth and graceful. Sentence about neck: Strong, but usually hidden by colorful neckerchief.

12. **Body:** <u>Obese, slim, chunky, solid, lanky:</u> Lean and hard, muscled. Sentence about body: Tough as rawhide without an ounce of fat.

13. **Hands and Arms:** <u>Long, short, hairy, wrinkled:</u> long or stubby fingers; cared-for, dirty, broken nails. Strong tanned hands and smooth arms, nails meticulously cut and kept clean in spite of toil and soil. Sentence description: Hands callused from honest work but gentle enough to hold a newborn colt or frightened bird.

14. **Legs and Feet:** <u>Long/short, fat/slim, attractive/misshapen:</u> Slim feet at the end of slightly bowed, medium-length sturdy legs. Descriptive sentence: It always amazed folks how fast Andy's legs could move when he raced away from danger or to someone else's rescue.

15. **One sentence describing the most outstanding physical feature of this character:** Andy Cullen's eyes lit up like twin Christmas candles when something pleased him, so bright you felt you could warm your hands at their glow.

CHARACTER JOB APPLICATION, page 2

8. Skin: Color, texture, soft, weather-beaten, smooth, pocked, wrinkled:
Sentence about skin: _____

_____

9. Mouth: Size, shape, thin/full lips, cupid's bow, pale, lipsticked, crooked,
cracked or smooth lips, usual expression_____
Teeth: Even, crooked, color, any missing. Sentence about mouth/teeth:

_____

_____

10. Shape of face: Round, oval, heart-shaped, square._____Sentence
about face:_____

_____

11. Neck: Scrawny, Wrinkled, graceful, smooth, strong._____
Sentence about neck:_____

_____

12. Body: Obese, slim, chunky, solid, lanky. _____Sentence about
body _____

_____

13. Hands and Arms: Long, short, hairy, wrinkled; long or stubby fingers;
cared-for, dirty, broken nails._____
Sentence description: _____

_____

14. Legs and Feet: Long/short, fat/slim, attractive/misshapen: _____
Descriptive sentence_____

_____

**15. One-two sentences describing the most outstanding physical feature
of this character:**_____

_____

_____

_____

CHARACTER JOB APPLICATION, example, page 3

Part II: Biography

1. **Birthdate/Birthplace:** (If place is to be featured in story, how well do I know it?) January 5, 1873, the Tonto Basin in Arizona. I have traveled in and researched the area for years. **Note:** Andy Cullen first appeared in my western novel *"Music in the Mountains"* as a secondary character, so I had done enough of the chart to meet the needs that role required.

2. **Parents:** Died when Andy was 15; not relevant except in teachings.

3. **Social class:** Social class in frontier Arizona spread wide enough to include everyone. Andy's cowboy skills win admiration and jobs.

4. **Full description of home, physical, emotional, spiritual:** Like other pioneer families, Andy lived in a simple cabin furnished with hand-made furniture, few luxuries but an abundance of love. Respect for God and hard work prevailed. **Note**: I rely a lot on encyclopedia pictures.

5. **Educational background:** Reading, writing and arithmetic + range lore.

6. **Work experience:** Riding, roping, rounding up cattle.

7. **Value system:** Higher than Andy knows, due to early training.

8. **Brother/sisters, position in family of character and how it has affected character:** Andy is the only twig on his family tree. It makes his desire to be part of a family strong. It has also made him self reliant.

9. **Atmosphere of home:** <u>warm, loving, secure, fearful, angry, bitter, sad</u>: Warm and loving, sometimes fearful that want would prevail.

10. **Surroundings:** <u>city, woods, farm:</u> Green valley beneath mighty cliff. **Does character stay/leave home? Why?** Leaves to chase wild horses.

11. **Sentence about character's background:** Andy Cullen is a product of his times; adventurous, but sound and firm as a pinyon nut.

CHARACTER JOB APPLICATION, page 3

Part II: Biography

1. **Birthdate/Birthplace:** _____

2. **Parents**:_____

_____

_____

3. **Social class:** _____

_____

4. **Full description of home, physical, emotional, spiritual:** _____

_____

_____

_____

_____

5. **Educational background:** _____

6. **Work experience:**_____

7. **Value system:** _____

8. **Brother/sisters, position in family of character and how it has affected character:** _____

_____

9. **Atmosphere of home:** warm, loving, secure, fearful, angry, bitter, sad.

_____

10. **Surroundings:** city, woods, farm, desert._____

 Does character stay/leave home? Why?_____

11. **Sentence about character's background:** _____

_____

_____

_____

CHARACTER JOB APPLICATION, example, page 4

Part III, Personal Information

1. **Basic Nature:** <u>moody, sullen, happy, hyper, easily led, stubborn:</u> Explain. Happy, but will fight any injustice toward man or beast.

2. **Sense of humor--what kind:** Loves a good joke but isn't malicious.

3. **Deepest dream/highest ambition:** Someday have his own spread, but not until *after* he catches Sheik, the magnificent black stallion.

4. **Belief in God or supreme power, to what extent.** Absolutely but hasn't done any committing.

5. **Determination to succeed/willingness to work:** Andy doggedly refuses to give up his quest; will work his boots off to gain his dream.

6. **Best friend(s)/husband, wife.** Smokey Travis and Columbine Ames *(from "Music in the Mountains")* plus his chestnut mare Chinquapin.

7. **Enemies and why:** Dunn, crooked rancher, after the wild horses.

8. **Hobbies, pastimes:** Ride, rope, race, chase the wild horse band.

9. **Reading/art/music preferences:** Doesn't read much; likes sunrises, sunsets and birdsongs, plus the cry of coyotes, wolves, etc.

10. **Dress/colors:** Cowboy garb, tans/browns, bright neckerchiefs.

11. **Personal creed:** Live clean, honest and square.

12. **Mannerisms:** Eyes crinkle at corners when he laughs; he says ain't.

13. **Smoke/drink/use drugs:** No. **Health:** Superb from his work.

14. **Best thing that has happened so far:** Meeting Columbine Ames and being able to help her escape from her stepfather so she can marry Smokey Travis of the Double J ranch near Flagstaff. Columbine's appeal to Andy's chivalry helped a great deal in changing boy to man.

CHARACTER JOB APPLICATION, page 4

Part III, Personal Information

1. Basic Nature:_____

2. Sense of humor--what kind:_____

3. Deepest dream/highest ambition:_____

_____

4. Belief in God or supreme power, to what extent. _____

_____

5. Determination to succeed/willingness to work:_____

_____

6. Best friend(s)/husband, wife:_____

_____

7. Enemies and why:_____

_____

8. Hobbies, pastimes:_____

9. Reading/art/music preferences:_____

10. Dress/colors:_____

11. Personal creed:_____

12. Mannerisms:_____

13. Smoke/drink/use drugs: ____Health: _____

14. Best thing that has happened so far: _____

_____

_____

CHARACTER JOB APPLICATION, example, page 5

15. **Worst thing:** Being held up on his way to Moab, Utah and having his supplies stolen.

16. **(a) Sees self as... (b) Is seen by others as...** (a) A poor lonesome cowpoke. (b) A mischief-loving but top range hand.

17. **Present problem:** Having to forsake his quest for Sheik.

18. **How it gets better or worse:** His spooked horse heads for parts unknown.

19. **Job Performance:** <u>How well does character relate to people of different ages, co-workers, friends, family. How well does he/she take direction/supervise others, etc</u>. Andy's cheerful smile and shock of tousled corn-colored hair make him a favorite. More important, his willingness to do more than his share and his range lore and skills win admiration and respect.

20. **Is character traditional/innovative/far out.** Quite traditional but also highly creative when the need arises.

21. **Self control:** Average plus. **Self discipline:** Same. **Judgment:** Normally good. **Ability to act in emergency situations:** Excellent.

Part IV: Special Qualifications

1. **Why is character worth writing about:** He typifies the best of the young riders who helped so much in settling the West.

2. **Strengths and weaknesses:** He has a great attitude toward life and is willing to work hard to get what he wants. Strength <u>and</u> weakness, Andy is so loyal it sometimes blinds him to the truth.

3. **How character differs from similar ones in stories/books and what sets him apart?** He's mature for his age but teachable. His joy of living and appreciation of nature and creation also make him different.

CHARACTER JOB APPLICATION, page 5

15. Worst thing:_____
_____

16. (a) Sees self as... (b) Is seen by others as..._____
_____

17. Present problem:_____
_____

18. How it gets better/worse:_____
_____

19. Job Performance: How well does character relate to people of different ages, co-workers, friends, family. How well does he/she take direction/supervise others, etc._____
_____
_____
_____

20. Is character traditional/innovative/far out:_____
_____

21. Self control: _____**Self discipline:**_____**Judgment:** _____**Ability to act in emergency situations:**_____

Part IV: Special Qualifications

1. Why is character worth writing about:_____
_____

2. Strengths and weaknesses:_____
_____

3. How character differs from similar ones in stories/books and what sets him or her apart?_____
_____

CHARACTER JOB APPLICATION, example, page 6

4. **Why does this character deserve this position?** Andy Cullen has simply been himself.

5. **Do I like/dislike character? Why? Will readers like/dislike? Why? Will they be for or against him? Why?** I like him and so will readers because he is vulnerable in spite of his insouciance. They will be for him simply because he deserves to win. He is appealing, real and will remind people of someone special they know and admire.

6. **What flaw keeps character from being too perfect _or_ what virtue keeps character from being too evil?** *Note: The best characters are not 100% good or evil any more than people. To make believable, combine traits.* Andy's judgment is sometimes clouded by loyalty and his usually well kept temper flares like a match to tinder.

7. **What trait will bring character most alive?** His unswerving determination to capture the wild stallion Sheik.

8. **Everyone has a secret. What is his/hers?** His love for a girl he fears will die in spite of everyone's best efforts.

9. **Everyone has some kind of handicap: physical, mental, spiritual or emotional. What handicaps your character?** His too-soft heart that permits no standing aside when anyone/anything is hurt or needs help.

10. **Single greatest influence on character and why.** Columbine Ames, whose trust called out the best a young man had to offer. Later in *"Captives of the Canyon"* another girl does the same.

11. **If applying for secondary role, is character so strong he/she will be more appealing and overshadow the lead?** N/A--he is the hero. **Note:** This can't be allowed to happen. If it does, disqualify this character from this story/book and use as the lead in another.

12. **What kind of neighbor would character make? Why?** Great, he'd be there if or when needed, no questions asked.

CHARACTER JOB APPLICATION, page 6

4. Why does this character deserve this position?_____

_____

_____

_____

5. Do I like/dislike character? Why? Will readers like/dislike? Why? Will they be for or against him? Why?_____

_____

_____

_____

6. What flaw keeps character from being too perfect _or_ what virtue keeps character from being too evil? Note: The best characters are not 100% good or evil any more than people. To make believable, combine traits._____

_____

7. What trait will bring character most alive?_____

_____

8. Everyone has a secret. What is his/hers?_____

_____

9. Everyone has some kind of handicap: physical, mental, spiritual or emotional. What handicaps your character? _____

_____

10. Single greatest influence on character and why._____

_____

_____

11. If applying for secondary role, is character so strong he/she will be more appealing and overshadow the lead?_____

12. What kind of neighbor would character make? Why?_____

_____

CHARACTER JOB APPLICATION, example, page 7

13. **One line characterization:** Andy Cullen looked life in the face--
    and grinned.

14. **Symbol that expresses character:** A singing lariat.

15. **Is character more saint or sinner?** Neither. Just a sometimes-wild
    cowboy who needs a good girl.

16. **How much of you is in character? What effect has character had
    on you as an author?** Quite a bit of the mischievous side of me. Andy
    has made me chuckle and a few times, blink back tears.

17. **Is character based on a real person, someone you admire, despise,
    etc.** A composition of many cowboy heroes with my own touches.

18. **Do you have a clear image of this character now?** Yes. (If not, go
    back and see if some questions need expanded answers.)

19. **A few adjectives that best describe character, such as steady,
    skunky, etc.** Steady, trustworthy, appealing, happy-go-lucky.

20. **Why will readers remember this character?** For his fight against
    tremendous, seemingly impossible odds.

FINAL QUESTION: **DOES THIS CHARACTER GET THIS JOB?
Why or why not?** Yes! He earned it with all of the above.

TIPS:
- **Never toss a character chart.** You will want or need them later.
- If character doesn't get this job, someday he or she will get another.
- **Always name characters immediately.** "He, she, the girl, or the
  old man" are nobodies and readers can't relate. Connie or
  Pablo or Jamal or Pete immediately assume identity.
- **Don't even consider including most of this chart in your story or
  book.** The information is to make you feel, see, suspect and think
  the way your characters do so you can bring them to life.

CHARACTER JOB APPLICATION, page 7

13. **One line characterization:**_____

_____

14. **Symbol that expresses character:** _____

15. **Is character more saint or sinner?**_____

_____

16. **How much of <u>you</u> is in character? What effect has character had on you as an author?**_____

_____

17. **Is character based on a real person, someone you admire, despise, other?**_____

18. **Do you have a clear image of this character now?** _____(If not, go back and see if some questions need expanded answers.)

19. **A few adjectives that best describe character, such as steady, skunky, etc.**_____

20. **Why will readers remember this character?**_____

_____

FINAL QUESTION: **Does this character get this job? Why/why not?**

_____

_____

Congratulations! You've completed one of the toughest assignments in TWW. You're ready to write the first draft of your story, if you haven't already done so.

Once the draft is done, go to PART 8: LEARNING TO EDIT and begin polishing. **Don't submit your story until you have completed all of the Part 8 lessons.**

ANALYSIS OF FILLED-IN CHARACTER CHART

Most of my character chart answers are self-explanatory. Following are reasons why I filled in certain blanks with these particular answers. It's important to know *why* our characters are as they are so we can convey that to our readers.

Andy Cullen, Part 1: Physical

In order to be credible as a wild horse hunter, Andy is presented as a product of his times: an orphaned young man just leaving his teens. He lives in a harsh land that has little time for gentleness. He must convince readers he can handle a task no one else has accomplished so far: the capture and taming of the wild black stallion Sheik.

Andy is no super-hero. Neither is he a weakling. He is simply himself, a lovable boy who tackles a man's job and matures in the process. Wild as the desert wind, tough as sagebrush, he also has a sunrise-soft side to his personality. It appeals to those with whom he works and rides, as well as the frail girl who enters his life.

His physical description is matched to his surroundings. He has been shaped by them into the strength needed for survival in the rugged canyon and mesa country. He has seen the mighty hand of his Creator in fire and flood, thunder and lightning. He knows the country's every capricious mood and stands in awe. His heart is prepared for love.

15. Most people have one outstanding physical feature. So should characters. It helps readers "see" them.

Part II: Biography

Don't beat readers over the head with historical information but do use what's needed. Each of these questions helps you get a more complete picture of Andy and how his background has molded him.

Part III: Personal
This section requires hard work but once it's done, you'll be inside your

character and discover what makes that person tick. Much of this information doesn't appear in my novel but investing a lot of time getting to know Andy before I began writing saved me countless hours of staring at my story muttering, "Great. What would he do now?"

Part IV: Special Qualifications

This final section is designed to make you struggle! However, the end result will be worth it. You'll have memorable characters who can handle their jobs.

If you've ever put together a jigsaw puzzle, you know how difficult it is to find just the right piece for every space. You also know how disastrous it is to try and shove pieces in where they don't fit. It's the same with the tough questions in this section. Forcing your characters to qualify for jobs means delving into the secret recesses of their hearts and minds.

3. The danger of Andy being a smudged carbon copy of other likable young cowboys meant real soul-searching. If I had admitted he really wasn't different, I couldn't have used him. Andy deserves to be remembered. He wouldn't be if I hadn't given him qualities that made him a cut above his companions by struggling with the questions.

8. **Knowing the secret fear** Andy carries helped me show Andy's vulnerability as well as his strengths and get readers on his side.

14. **Symbols are important.** Branding irons for outlaws, scalpels for doctors/nurses, well-worn Bibles for ministers add significance.

16. Reminder: **If your characters are too autobiographical** you'll run into problems. Changing anything from the way it actually was may be difficult and getting a story/novel turned down may be shattering. The rejection of fictional characters is one thing; yourself, another.

20. Unless you have a strong answer to this, lay aside the chart and either
    (1) wait until you can come up with a valid answer, or
    (2) save this character and create another.

FINAL QUESTION/ANSWER: **Andy got the job because he earned it.**

PART 6: Books

THE ANATOMY OF A NOVEL is much like that of a short story

Three is Key: **Novels start with:**
—an <u>i</u>nteresting individual
—an <u>i</u>nspiring setting, <u>or</u>
—an <u>i</u>ntriguing incident

They present 3 c's	**They contain:**	**A good breakdown**
—a strong <u>c</u>haracter	—an appealing beginning	—1/3 <u>h</u>ook*
—in meaningful <u>c</u>onflict	—an attention-holding middle	—1/3 <u>h</u>old**
—resulting in <u>c</u>hange	—a satisfying ending	—1/3 <u>h</u>ighlights
		***

 *HOOK introduces character(s); sets stage; introduces first problem.

 **HOLD develops characters; alternates obstacles and temporary victories.

***HIGHLIGHTS presents crisis (**black moment when all seems lost and the problem must be faced**); lead character's choice; conclusion showing how lead character changed because of that choice.

<u>Example:</u> A 45,000 word novel (roughly 180 double spaced, typed pages) would have approximately 60 pages/15,000 words per "H." **Don't be concerned if your book doesn't match exactly.** These are suggested breakdowns only.

To sell, novels must:
♦ **adhere to publishers' word lengths** (see <u>Word Lengths</u> in Appendix)
♦ **keep readers intrigued/interested so they will go on reading**
♦ **have good subplots as well as the main storyline**
♦ **avoid too many viewpoints (I normally alternate chapters or sections between my hero and heroine's viewpoint.)**

Novels also consist of:
♦ <u>dialogue</u> to move plot forward, bridge time gaps and share insight
♦ short, blended-in <u>description</u>; strong verbs add color
♦ <u>narration</u>, simple storytelling interspersed with dialogue/description

THE ANATOMY OF A NONFICTION BOOK
is similar to that of articles

What's hot in nonfiction books:

♦ **How to** if you have new information or a fresh approach. Be sure to know what's already out there before writing your book.

♦ **Personal experience** if it's dramatic, bizarre or unique enough to beat the competition from all the books written by well-known personalities. Recovery books have glutted the market. If you wish to sell an "overcoming" book it will need to focus on what you learned rather than the process of recovering from bad or tragic situations.

♦ **A better life** for you. If you have experiences and knowledge that can offer readers a higher quality of living, you may find a publisher.

♦ **Inspirational/religious.** Fresh, new insights into scripture; devotionals continue to be popular. Again, *know your competition.*

♦ **Cookbooks** with a twist that can serve to sell them.

♦ **Limited word gift books**, such as "Life's Little Instruction Book."

♦ Many others, including technical. Check a market guide category Index.

Tips:

1. A great percentage of nonfiction books are sold on the basis of a strong proposal, Table of Contents and sample chapters. (Part 7: Marketing). This package should be as professional and complete as you   can make it.

2. It is just as important to hook novel and nonfiction book readers as it is when you're writing articles/short stories. Editors frankly state they read the first two paragraphs of a short manuscript, the first page plus only as many others as hold their interest of book length manuscripts. Saving the "good stuff" for chapters 2, 10 and 17 may well mean it won't be read.

Hook, hold, highlight—to keep editors and readers reading.

NOVEL OUTLINE, example, page 1

1. **Proposed title/why/approx. length:** *CAPTIVES OF THE CANYON.*
   Refers to legend of Dead Horse Point, near Moab, Utah. 45,000+ words.

2. **Markets:** Publishers of historical novels, westerns. (Written for HEART-SONG PRESENTS: 4th/final in the Western Trails Quartet: *Silence in the Sage, Whispers in the Wilderness and Music in the Mountains.)*

3. **Lead/important secondary characters:** Andy Cullen from "Music"; Linnet Allen of Boston; Judd and George Allen, Linnet's father and brother, co-owners of the Rocking A; Silas Dunn, crooked rancher; Sarah Salt, Reddy Hode, Tommy Blake, Charlie Moore work on Rocking A.
   See: "Quick Reference" chart, in Appendix, a good way to keep track.

4. **Theme:** *(one-sentence underlying message)*:Miracles come in many ways.

5. **Plot** (*brief synopsis*): Wild-horse hunter cowboy meets Eastern girl who is visiting in Moab. She furnishes him with a second dream: to help her regain her health then win her love--along with capturing the wild black stallion Sheik he has chased for so long.

6. **Lead character's problem at beginning of story:** He's in the middle of following Sheik and gets held up by masked raiders who steal his supplies.

7. **How it gets better or worse:** His spooked horse leaves him stranded.

8. **Obstacles/temporary victories:** Andy is robbed. He learns he isn't the only one after Sheik and his band of mares. Doctor says Linnet can't live. Horses need defense against local cowboys and ranchers. Dead Horse Point becomes a challenge to the daring cowboy. So does Linnet.

9. **Setting and time period:** Frontier Arizona and Utah, early 1890's.
   Target readership: 10-110, male and female.

10. **Why are you writing this novel?:** Legend of the area fascinates me. I also thoroughly enjoyed Andy Cullen in "Music." He convinced me he'd be perfect as the hero in *"Captives of the Canyon."*

NOVEL OUTLINE, page 1

1. Proposed title/why/approx. length:_____
_____

2. Markets: _____

3. Lead/important secondary characters: _____
_____
_____
_____

4. Theme: (one-sentence underlying message)**:** _____
_____

5. Plot (brief synopsis)**:** _____
_____
_____
_____

6. Lead character's problem at beginning of story: _____
_____
_____

7. How it gets better or worse: _____
_____

8. Obstacles/temporary victories: _____
_____
_____
_____

9. Setting and time period:_____
 Target readership:_____

10. Why are you writing this story?:_____
_____
_____

NOVEL OUTLINE, example, page 2

11. **What qualifies you to write this story:** I know the area well through visiting, extensive research and a lifelong love affair with the West.

12. **How lead character will change during story:** From happy-go-lucky carefree cowboy to a mature man concerned about others.

13. **Opening sentences:** The horrid scream of a terrified animal split the frosty morning air. The beating of wings followed. Andy Cullen, Arizona cowboy who had ridden into Utah in search of a legendary black stallion bent forward in the saddle. "Yippee-ay! It's him, old girl!"

14. **Surprise or twist/Clues planted:** The saving of two horses. Andy's a great horseman and loves animals.

15. **Possible closing sentences:** Even as the yawning canyon had claimed its captives, Linnet—and God—laid claim to Andy's heart. Yet somewhere far from saddle and corral... (Begin/end changed drastically.)

16. **How it differs from other similar titles:** I know of no other books that deal with the legend of Dead Horse Point. Zane Grey's "*Wild Horse Mesa*" is perhaps the closest and *"Captives"* is nothing like it.

17. **Why an editor will buy and readers will remember:** It completes the quartet. Readers will remember the poignant fights of brave characters.

18. **What feeling you want to leave with readers:** Refusing to give up goes hand in hand with many kinds of miracles.

19. **Does the planned ending fit? Will readers find it acceptable?:** Very much so; the final twist is believable and satisfying.

20. **Is the book one you would check out of the library or buy?:** You bet! It offers a hard-hitting, exciting story without pages of profanity and rivers of blood.

Note: *Before* you start writing your novel, do your character charts and "Brainstorming/Chapter Highlights" chart (page 63).

NOVEL OUTLINE, page 2

11. **What qualifies you to write this story:**_____

_____

12. **How lead character will change during story:**_____

_____

13. **Opening sentences:**_____

_____

_____

_____

14. **Surprise or twist/Clues planted:** _____

_____

15. **Possible closing sentences:** _____

_____

_____

_____

16. **How it differs from similar titles:** _____

_____

_____

17. **Why an editor will buy and readers will remember:** _____

_____

18. **What feeling you want to leave with readers:**_____

_____

19. **Does the planned ending fit? Will readers find it acceptable?:**_____

_____

20. **Is the book one you would check out of the library or buy?:**_____

_____

Note: *Before* you start writing your novel, do your character charts and
a"Brainstorming/Chapter Highlights" chart (page 63).

ANALYSIS OF NOVEL OUTLINE

1. Examples of **titles** and sample **beginnings** given on pages 67-68. Length was chosen to match the other titles in the series.

2. I had the advantage of knowing this would go to a particular place. With other titles, I diligently study market listings and guidelines. It is far better to aim toward a field with several possible publishers than to target one specific place on the chance you can sell to them.

3-4. Self-explanatory.

5. **Condensing** your entire plot into capsule form is excellent discipline.

6-7. Self-explanatory.

8. "**Chapter Highlights**" chart (page 62) shows how I brainstormed to come up with crises, special events, etc.

9. I **never choose** a setting or time period that:
   (a) I don't know well from being there or experiencing it, **or**
   (b) that I can't research thoroughly.
   My exacting father could spot a historical or setting error immediately and often refused to read books that showed authors hadn't done their homework. He taught me the **importance of details**. Once Mom and I spent hours researching how far Evangeline (in *"Angel of the North"*) could travel by train in early 1900's Canada and where she'd have to change to canoe or snowshoes. Accuracy is one reason I have readers from ages 10-100+, of both sexes.

10. There are many **valid reasons to write a novel**. You may write for the sheer love of writing, for money, to be read, from the deep conviction it needs to be written, to influence others, etc. All my work is written to help make this world a better place and to offer inspirational alternatives to the reams of questionable literature available. I saw in this setting and legend the possibility of a thoroughly enjoyable novel that would also inspire. Result: The book *Captives of the Canyon.*

11. Self-explanatory.

12. Back to the 3 c's: **character** in **conflict** resulting in **change**. Andy is not the same person at the end of the story as in the beginning. His growing recognition throughout the book concerning the claim others have on him as a member of the human race makes him responsible and mature.

13. In the **planning stages**, this opening seemed perfect. It wasn't. It actually ended up about twenty pages into the novel and fit there like a pigskin glove. I needed to introduce Andy, plant clues, build suspense and get readers rooting for him before this scene could work most effectively.

14. **Twists, turns, quirks**; clues planted to be fair with readers. All take a lot of planning. The fact that readers know how much Andy loves horses and the extent of his skill makes later happenings believable.

15. **Closing sentences** also changed completely, yet carried the same general flavor as those originally planned. My endings must satisfy me or they are rewritten as many times as it takes to do so. In *"Captives,"* the beauty of a rider's life changed by his experiences shines with every hard-chosen word.

16. Self-explanatory.

17. I had the advantage of it being part of a **series** so didn't have to fret about marketing. I did need to present struggles real enough to make an impact.

18. Too many folks sit around waiting for God or life to make their **dreams** come true. I wanted to point out we need to do our part.

19. "Acceptable" in this case means happy, but a bittersweet happiness. The majority of readers/editors today lean toward happy endings. They will settle for hopeful ones that aren't necessarily happy but that fit. It is not impossible (but it is harder) to sell **novels that end on a tragic note**. I stick mainly to happy endings but am not afraid to add a haunting quality to a story's close, as with *"Music."*

20. **I only write the kinds of books I like to read again and again.**

Brainstorming/Chapter Highlights Chart, example

•Andy Cullen leaves Utah to chase the legendary black stallion Sheik.

•He is held up and provisions are stolen. His horse spooks. He's left stranded miles from Moab.

•Horse returns.

•Andy stumbles across Sheik, caught in a small slide. Andy must free him and win trust.

•Back East, frail Linnet Allen rebels when she's told she can't live. She persuades her father to take her out West to the Rocking A ranch Judd and his brother own.

•Linnet forces herself to eat and improve enough to travel.

•Sheer grit and enchantment keep her going until she reaches the Rocking A.

•She begins a series of faltering steps toward health, sustained by the feeling it isn't her time to die.

•A meeting with Andy. Far-reaching effects. He offers Linnet

cheerful belief she can be well. She shares her faith in God.

•Capture and taming of Sheik

•Relapse for Linnet.

•Confrontation with crooked rancher Dunn and outlaw partners.

•Celebration and horse race.

•A wild horse drive.

•A shooting.

•A bad time for Andy.

•An indelible, black spot on the history of Utah territory.

•Linnet's valiant struggle against poor health since childhood.

•Uncle George and Sarah Salt's refusal to give up.

•Cowboys' admiration for the plucky Eastern girl.

•A pitch-black night of terror.

•Growing love between Andy and Linnet.

•Improvements in her health.

•Overcoming evil on the range.

•A poignant and surprising gift.

BRAINSTORMING/CHAPTER HIGHLIGHTS CHART

NONFICTION BOOK OUTLINE, example

Before beginning a nonfiction book, check *BOOKS IN PRINT* to see how many are already available on your subject and how yours will differ.

1. **Title/ Subject/Length:** *Writing Smarter, not harder, The Workbook Way.* Title/subject self-explanatory. 25,000-30,000 words

2. **Markets, 6-10:** Any company that does writing books.

3. **One sentence theme:** Using *The Workbook Way* increases output, saves time, gives direction and makes writing easier/more enjoyable.

4. **Other books on subject/how mine differs:** There are shelves of books on writing but they aren't based on my ***"pre-write," don't rewrite*** system.

5. **Brief synopsis:** The unique charting approach that allows me to write pro-lifically and sell extensively is shared. Writers are walked through getting the idea, developing and polishing it, to contacting an editor. Everything is shown through filled-in examples, graphic presentations, etc.

6. **Why are you qualified to write it? Why are you writing it?:** It works for me and is working for hundreds of my college and workshop writing students. First developed for self and students, others can also benefit.

7. **Supports used:** Quotes X , Anecdotes X ; Documented facts X ; llustrations/examples X ; Practical suggestions X ; Dialogue X; Personal experiences: good examples of how X /how *not* X to do it.

8. **What can readers "take away"?:** The fact there's a lot better way to write than just beginning when an idea strikes plus solid information about writing both well and salably.

9. **Why should an editor buy it?:** Who can resist a spanking new workbook's clean, white pages? It invites writers to carry it with them and fill-in during lunch breaks, waiting at the doctor's office, etc. *The Workbook Way* responds to the joke: "How do you eat an elephant?" By encouraging writers to write their manuscripts, "one bite at a time."

NONFICTION BOOK OUTLINE, example

Before beginning a nonfiction book, check *BOOKS IN PRINT* to see how many are already available on your subject and how yours will differ.

1. Title/ Subject/Length:_____
_____

2. Markets, 6-10: _____
_____

3. One sentence theme: _____
_____

4. Other books on subject/how mine differs: _____
_____
_____

5. Brief synopsis:_____
_____
_____
_____

6. Why are you qualified to write it? Why are you writing it?_____
_____

7. Supports used: Quotes_____; Anecdotes_____; Documented facts_____; llustrations/examples_____; Practical suggestions_____; Dialogue_____; Personal experiences--good examples of how ___ /how *not* to do it_____.

8. What can readers "take away"? _____
_____

9. Why should an editor buy it?_____
_____
_____
_____

Do a "Brainstorming/Chapter Highlights" chart (pages 62-63)

ANALYSIS OF NONFICTION BOOK OUTLINE

1. Self-explanatory.

2. Choose the **markets that are doing something similar** to what you have to offer or that list in their guidelines they will consider your type manuscript.

3. Do type your **theme** and paste it by your work area where you can refer to it often. This helps you **stay in focus**.

4. It doesn't pay to ignore what's out there. You need to **examine competition** then inform editor why your book is different and worthwhile.

5. Sometimes an editor wants an extremely **brief synopsis** with which to approach fellow editors, the marketing department, etc. Editors also see in your synopsis **possible dust jacket blurbs**--those come-on type introductions on the back or inside the front cover.

6. I want more persons to benefit from the unique, innovative system of writing that has helped me to accumulate 93 book contracts and 1200+ story/article sales in less than 20 years of writing.

7. The greater the **variety of supports** you use in your nonfiction book, the better. If it's technical, you'll quote a lot of documented facts. TWW is more informal. Its anecdotes, examples, suggestions, dialogue, etc. make it fun reading and help to take the pain out of learning.

8. Nonfiction books must have far greater **"takeaway"** than novels. Readers need to learn new things, be motivated to practice what the book presented. (Please, no preaching. Let the book's examples, etc. do that for you.)

9. You need to figure this one out by extensive **market and library research.** I checked and to my joy, found nothing like TWW. Some hardback books do have questions, exercises, etc. None of them offer **the promise**, *"I'll take your hand, walk you down the rough and rocky road to authorship I so fearfully traveled. I'll show you the boulders I stumbled over, obstacles that discourage even those with God-given talent and cause them to give up."*

TITLES AND BEGINNINGS

First impressions can be lasting. That's why it's so important to impress an editor immediately. Two good ways to do this: offer **terrific titles** and **irresistible beginnings.**

Choose **titles** that are meaningful to each particular manuscript. Many times your subject will indicate the best title. At other times, you may take it from a phrase in the book. I choose my title before ever starting the book. That way I can work it (or its message) in as a natural part of the story.

Your **opening paragraphs** must grab editors and readers without being an obvious ploy. "Smiling, the girl fell dead" will attract attention but many editors dislike such a blatant attempt to do so.

—The following actual beginnings show different approaches—

Presenting a place/mood, example

Seattle fog curled into the city's streets like a kitten twined around a beloved owner's legs.

Wisps and drifts softened street lights and muted brilliant piles of autumn leaves waiting to be gathered and recycled. The mournful howl of a Puget Sound ferry coming in from Bainbridge Island added an eerie touch and reminded Seattle's inhabitants Halloween lurked just a few days away. (Prologue, contemporary nurse/doctor/hospital novel *Lamp in Darkness,* Heartsong Presents, division of Barbour Books)

Hint of intrigue/promise, example

For a single moment she saw his face--etched against the lurid light of flickering flames.
    She never forgot.
    Twenty years later, she saw his face again--limned against a sun-glorified stained glass window.
    She never forgot. (Prologue, contemporary nurse novel *Flickering Flames* (sequel to *Lamp in Darkness,* Heartsong Presents)

Dialogue, example

"Terri, do you think Tante Theresa is—uh, all there?"
    The question from her twin brother was so unexpected it all but rocked Terri off her perch. (Chapter 1, juvenile, *The Mysterious Treadle Machine,* Review and Herald Publishers)

BEGINNINGS, examples

Introduce character/touch on setting/present problem example

Footsore and weary, Andy Cullen paused in the endless pursuit of his chestnut mare Chinquapin and surveyed the world around him with disfavor. "Doggone it, why'd I ever leave the Double J?" he complained to a buzzard sailing overhead, bent on its grisly mission. Yet even his sour mood couldn't erase the joy of living that evidenced itself in sparkling brown eyes and a grin like the crack in a cheap watermelon. A lock of hair darkened by sweat from its normal ripe corn color dangled over his forehead. Andy shoved it back under his Stetson then mopped his face with a bright red neckerchief. He eyed the crowding red rock walls that towered above him and offered a million hiding places for a frightened horse. "Chinq, at least they didn't get you."

(In this opening we: meet Andy; learn he's following his runaway horse; get a quick physical description; discover he has a normally happy disposition; catch a glimpse of his surroundings and find out someone robbed him but didn't get Chinq. The next paragraphs tell more:)

He limped to a nearby boulder the size of a house and leaned against it, glad for shade.

"Lord, if you're real the way Columbine and Smokey believe, I could sure use a hand. This southeastern Utah ain't no place for a cowpoke on foot a million miles from nowhere. No water. No canteen. Nothing but red and orange rocks."

He shuddered. He hadn't minded their presence while riding through. Alone, hungry and thirsty, they posed a serious threat--not only to his quest but his life.

"I reckon You help those who help themselves," he muttered and straightened. High-heeled boots raised him taller than his 5'9". He stretched muscled arms. Every sinew in his body ached. Lean, stripling, seasoned, the unaccustomed walking all riders hated had taken its toll and Chinq had only been missing since last night.

Andy made a disgusted sound. How could he have been so careless? On the other hand, who'd expect a self-respecting outlaw band to be in a forsaken place like this? (Chapter 1, western novel, *Captives of the Canyon*, Heartsong Presents)

The calm before the storm, example

Thirteen-year-old Michael Hilton whistled his way toward home. (*For the Love of Mike*, Rev./Herald)

ENDINGS

Reminder: While beginnings invite, endings encourage readers to recommend your book to others or to reread it. Pay close attention to your final scene, paragraph, sentence. They are what will be remembered and in many ways, are the most important part of your story, article or book.

Titles correlating with "beginnings" on the previous two pages:

Lamp in Darkness refers back to the title and one of the most significant happenings in the story. A tall white candle, an old kerosene lamp and medical personnel who hold high the torch of their calling combine to bring the book full circle.

Flickering Flames is also full circle. A two-sentence Epilogue picks up some of the same wording used in the Prologue and another place in the story to tie up loose ends in a full-circle-with-a-quirk ending.

The Mysterious Treadle Machine gives the solution to the mystery of the old sewing machine and leaves readers satisfied with the outcome.

Music in the Mountains offers a believable ending that leaves readers with a smile and perhaps a longing to experience the pioneer way of life that is gone forever.

For the Love of Mike shows the maturity the young hero gained since his world fell apart less than two years earlier. His increased faith in himself and God give stability to the story.

Captives of the Canyon uses a few poignant sentences to tie up the hero's long search in a satisfying manner.

Mini-assignment:
⇒ Think of several books whose endings really got to you.
⇒ Decide why and strive for the same effect in your endings.

Part 7: Marketing

It's as important to know about marketing as it is to form good writing habits.

You need have no fear of approaching editors *if:*

- ♦ **you have carefully researched their needs**
- ♦ **you have something to offer within their scope**
      that has a new, fresh slant
- ♦ **you have developed your skills**
      through study and practice
- ♦ **you approach them professionally**

The following examples show a proven, successful way to contact editors. They include: (1) An idea **query** to see if editor is interested in your particular idea/approach. (2) A **Book Proposal** to go with sample chapters. (Don't send random chapters unless requested by an editor. They don't show your capability to sustain the story in a logical, believable way.) (3) A **cover letter** to accompany the proposal. **All these are adaptable to your specific needs.**

If you are pitching (marketing) a nonfiction book, you must also include a well-prepared **Table of Contents**, such as the one in this handbook.

A **checklist** for editor may go either on the bottom of your letter or on a self-addressed stamped postcard. (Review query info., pages 20-22.)

I can't advise sending book length manuscripts out to more than one publisher at the same time, even though some say they do accept **simultaneous submissions**. This practice can lead to problems. If two editors want the book, one is going to be unhappy at having invested many hours of editorial time only to learn you sold elsewhere. Scratch any chance of ever selling future manuscripts to that editor; also, word gets around in the publishing business.

I have no qualms about multiple queries and/or book proposals; they require far less consideration time. But **I always tell the editors** I am querying simultaneously and will submit singly.

SAMPLE NOVEL IDEA QUERY (see Appendix, 1½" margins)

(Your Letterhead)

August 20, 1993

Stephen Reginald Managing Editor
BARBOUR BOOKS
PO Box 719
Uhrichsville OH 44683

Dear Mr. Reginald:

Two years ago when I visited Dead Horse Point near Moab, Utah, the story of how it got its name fascinated and saddened me. Wild mustangs roamed the mesas before the turn of the century. The unique rock promontory provided a natural corral into which cowboys and ranchers drove the herd. The only escape lay in a narrow 30-yard neck of land. Once fenced, the horses were secured. Roped and broken, the better ones were kept for personal use or sold to Eastern markets, the culls ("broomtails") remained on the Point.

According to legend, a band of broomtails was left corralled. The gate was <u>supposedly</u> open so the wild horses could return to the open range. For some unknown reason, the mustangs stayed. They died of thirst within sight of the Colorado River 2000 feet below.

I am using this story and magnificent setting for a 45,000 word novel, *CAPTIVES OF THE CANYON*, a colorful tale of the Old West. Andy Cullen (first introduced in *MUSIC IN THE MOUNTAINS*) is perfect in the role of wild horse hunter whose chief aim is to capture the legendary black stallion Sheik. Frail Linnet Allen, whose spirit and faith in God are strong enough to fight doctors' assurances she cannot live, is an appealing heroine. The poignant story of good and evil played out amidst red-rock mountains and canyons offers high action and a good read.

May I send Book Proposal and sample chapters? Thank you for your response.

Sincerely,

Enclosures: Resume/Booklist/SASE

_____Please send Proposal/sample chapters for *CAPTIVES OF THE CANYON*.
_____Overstocked. Try after_____
_____Sorry, not for us. Comments, if any_____
_____
Signed_____Date_____for BARBOUR BOOKS

SAMPLE NOVEL PROPOSAL (1½" margins, all sides)

(Your letterhead)

BOOK PROPOSAL

Title	**CAPTIVES OF THE CANYON**
By	Colleen L. Reece with Gary Dale (validates both western and romance aspects)
Type	Inspirational historical/western *
Length	45,000+ words
Status	Chapters 1-3 enclosed; remainder fully planned
Target completion date	Mid-December 1993
Interest level	Upper elementary through Senior Adult
Reading level	Upper elementary-Junior High
Setting/Time period	Moab, Utah/surrounding area; early 1890s
Theme	Miracles come in many ways.

Lead characters

ANDY CULLEN—lovable, mischievous, corn-colored shocky hair, glowing brown eyes and a penchant for adventure.

LINNET ALLEN—named for the small finch; an invalid who refuses to die in her Boston home without ever seeing the West she has dreamed of so long. Soft blue eyes, medium brown hair.

JUDD ALLEN—the kindest of fathers; has been mother as well since his wife died; believes God will spare Linnet.

GEORGE ALLEN—co-owner of the Rocking A ranch near Moab, Utah, along with Judd; runs it while Judd remains in the East.

SILAS DUNN—owner of the Bar D spread; questionable at best.

Story: *(Nonfiction should be outlined in chapters. Fiction can be either way.)*

Into the rugged country surrounding Moab, Utah comes Arizona cowboy Andy Cullen, in search of a legendary black stallion. Sheik lives up to his name by stealing mares from the local ranchers and driving away would-be rulers from his band. Andy's desire is to capture and tame Sheik, the grandest horse in the country—who may exist only

* Spin-off from *MUSIC IN THE MOUNTAINS*

Reece,Captives,2

in range gossip and campfire tales! Astride his faithful chestnut mare Chinquapin, nicknamed Chinq, Andy relentlessly pursues a band of horses across untold miles. They are a far cry from the Double J ranch near Flagstaff, Arizona where Andy hired on after delivering Columbine Ames to her sweetheart. Great red stone arches, pillars and fantastically designed structures leave him gaping. So does the point 6000 feet above sea level that finds him staring into a gorge similar to the Grand Canyon of the Colorado.

Tired, his usual good nature dimmed by loss of his money belt stolen by robbers, Andy's spirits rise when he discovers Sheik desperately trying to free himself from a small slide. The exultant cowboy must win the black's trust and help the terrified horse who fights every move.

. . .

Thousands of miles east, Linnet Allen faces the truth. She is going to die. A strong Christian, she tries to accept it as God's will--and rebels. She's been frail since childhood when the shock of her mother's death turned her into a ghost of the rosy child who pranced through her Boston home on imaginary steeds.

Linnet tries to have courage and comfort her father Judd but the spirit that once led her ancestors to flee persecution and settle in the New World a few crossings after the Mayflower rises in protest. Must she die before she has ever lived? Before she can journey West to the Rocking A ranch in Utah, co-owned by her Uncle George who runs it, and Linnet's father?

The proposal continues, following the information from the **Brainstorming/Chapter Highlights Chart Example** (page 62)

CAPTIVES OF THE CANYON is written in simple past tense. **The proposal is written in present tense** to give a feeling of action and being there, which is the proper way to write a Novel Book Proposal.

SAMPLE NONFICTION BOOK IDEA QUERY

(Set up on letterhead the same as the Sample Novel Query, page 71)

(Your letterhead)

Date

Editor
Address

Dear ... :

For some years I have been perfecting a manuscript based on my unique "pre-writing" method. The success of: *WRITING SMARTER, not harder, The Workbook Way,* is undeniable: 93 book contracts, 1200+ short manuscript sales in less than 20 years. (resume and booklist enclosed.) My college students are using it and selling. Popular authors/writing teachers/speakers such as Lauraine Snelling (*Golden Filly Series* and many other books, articles) plan to make it required text for their classes when TWW becomes available.

Most of my current juvenile and adult novels are with BARBOUR BOOKS, who aren't currently doing anything like this.

I am enclosing a mini-proposal and Table of Contents. May I send a complete Book Proposal with sample chapters? Thank you for your consideration and response.

Sincerely,

Enclosures: listed/SASE

_____Please send detailed proposal of TWW and first _____ chapters.

_____Maybe later. If still available, contact us after_____.

_____Sorry. Comments, if any_____

_____

_____

Signed_____Date_____for (<u>name of company</u>)

Mini-proposal on the next pages accompanies query and Table of Contents.

BOOK PROPOSAL
(see Appendix, 1½" margins)

(Your letterhead)

BOOK PROPOSAL

Title	***WRITING SMARTER, not harder, The Workbook Way***
By	Colleen L. Reece
Cover hook	This proven approach increases output and sales through "pre-writing" that helps eliminate rewriting
Status	In final revision
Length	Approx. 25,000-30,000 words; 100+ camera-ready pages plus Table of Contents and 3 page Introduction
Format	Soft cover workbook, 8 1/2" x 11"
Target market	Writers at all levels (Jr. High up) who wish to increase manuscript quality, output, sales or simply get started
Theme	Success speaks for itself.

What Makes *The Workbook Way* (TWW) Unique

Many good writing books assume readers have a certain amount of writing knowledge, i.e., writing jargon, how to set up manuscript pages, etc.
TWW assumes nothing.

Some tell how to perform tasks.
TWW shows, using the detailed charts that have enabled the author to accumulate 93 book contracts and 1200+ short sales in 20 years.

Many overwhelm with pages of solid type.
TWW asks readers not to begin manuscripts until they (1) complete a series of "pre-writing" charts; (2) study filled-in examples from author's published work and explanations on why they were completed that way.

Others can be hard to understand.
TWW is so simple author has used successfully with students ranging from upper elementary through senior adult. Many students have sold stories, articles and books by following this step-by-step method.

Some intimidate. (length, etc.)
TWW is writer friendly, to meet the needs of the small-town girl who still lives inside the author, who likes clear, simple directions and believes an example is worth a dozen pages of text.

Reece, TWW Proposal, 2

Special Features

WRITER'S DIGEST BOOKS labeled it, *unique, innovative, worthwhile*, but wouldn't go for the workbook format that keeps it from being just another writing book.) (I was a Writer's Digest School instructor for 15 years; they might include *Writing Smarter, not harder, The Workbook Way* in their book club.)

•**Handiness factor.** TWW offers a portable writing course. Busy persons can stuff it in a lunch bag or attaché case and fill in blanks during breaks or while on a bus, waiting in airports, doctor's or dentist's office. That way, actual writing time won't be consumed by just the preparation part.

• **Plan ahead approach** gets writer so on track and rooted in the manuscript that middle sag, boredom and discouragement are lessened.

• **Time-saving techniques** are valuable to both beginners and established authors

• **Learning to edit** your own work creates confidence; the many tips and extensive checklists help ensure accuracy and quality submissions.

• **"Once over lightly"** areas such as explanation of terms, etc., come with recommendations on where to get more information on the subject.

• **Method takes writers by the hand** and walks them from picking an idea to developing, polishing, querying, submitting and handling rejection.

TWW is especially helpful for those who--
      1. can't seem to get started or need to be better organized.
      2. have great beginnings, endings, or both, but fall apart in the middle.
      3. are overwhelmed by what it takes to complete a manuscript.
      4. long to make better use of their time and become more prolific.

TWW's Most Valuable Aspects

⇒ **The workbook format.** Who can resist the clean inviting pages of a workbook? Empty computer screens and white paper intimidate. Questions with blanks entice and encourage responses.

⇒ **TWW breaks mountain-size tasks** into small steps that bring writers closer to their goal: a finished manuscript. Every step also offers an important fringe benefit: satisfaction at having completed another portion of the task.

⇒ **Knowing the author has used it so successfully adds built-in appeal.**

BOOK PROPOSAL COVER LETTER, example
(sent after I receive the editor's permission to submit a proposal*)

(Your letterhead)

September 2, 1994

Stephen Reginald Managing Editor
HEARTSONG PRESENTS
PO Box 719
Uhrichsville OH 44683

Dear Mr. Reginald:

Thank you for permission to submit Book Proposal and sample chapters for
CAPTIVES OF THE CANYON. I am enclosing chapters 1-3.

I appreciate your consideration and look forward to your response.

Sincerely,

Enclosures: listed/SASE

_____Please send complete manuscript, CAPTIVES OF THE CANYON. * *
_____Maybe later. Try us again after_____
_____Sorry, this isn't for us. Comments, if any_____
_____
Signed_____Date_____for HEARTSONG PRESENTS

---

 * A slight variation of this basic cover letter accompanied the completed manuscript submitted on November 24, 1994.

** Note: Less experienced authors should have at least the first draft of a book completed or be *very sure* they can write it in a reasonable length of time before offering a project to an editor.

One of my **horror stories** is my first novel, *THE HERITAGE OF NURSE O'HARA*. I wrote one chapter and sent it to Avalon Books. Three days later I received a warm invitation to "please send the rest of the manuscript as soon as possible." I had no outline, no character charts and only hazy plans for the "rest of the manuscript!"

PART 8: Learning to Edit, with Exercise

You've done your charts. You've written your first draft. Now it's time to take a long hard look at how you can improve your story, book or article.

The single greatest thing you can learn from any book, class or teacher is how to edit your own work. TWW's checklists come from editor comments and market knowledge. They comprise about 99% of the most common writing errors. Many are "brands of beginners." Others infest even best-selling authors' work. Louis L'Amour and Victoria Holt's great books could be even better with fewer uses of the passive verbs *was* and *would*, respectively.

Mark of Our Moccasins is a small book issued by the Council For Indian Education, 1982 (serialized in *Lifeglow*) based on legends from my home town. It's a poignant story of a native American boy who learns to appreciate the uniqueness of his great-grandfather and his own rich heritage. Here is the opening:

"Leave school *now*? Miss graduation and everything I've worked for all these years?" Tom Jackson's face was angry. "Never! Grandfather must be crazy!"

"Walking Eagle is not crazy." The old man who came into the room was bent with the years of living, but his white head was held proudly. His dark eyes flashed. "Young Eagle will go with me."

"Sorry, grandfather." Tom faced the old man, his own dark eyes flashing. "I'm getting a scholarship to college at graduation. I wouldn't miss walking across that stage for anything in the world."

"It has been taken care of. You will get the paper later, Young Eagle."

"I'm not going!" Tom shut his teeth hard, then added, "And I wish you would call me Tom, like everyone else does!"

"Young Eagle will go with me. I have spoken." There was something grand about the old man as he left the room.

Tom dropped into a chair. "I *can't* go! I don't even want to. Why should I go off on this crazy trip? Or why can't he wait until after graduation? It's only a few weeks away!"

Edit this portion in any way you feel would improve it, before reading my revision.

Polished Version

"Leave school *now*? Miss graduation and everything I've worked for all these years?" Anger and disbelief flowed through Tom Jackson's body like the Skagit River in flood. "Grandfather must be crazy!"

"Walking Eagle is not crazy." The white-haired old man, bent from years of living, walked proudly into the room. His dark eyes flashed. "Young Eagle will go with me."

"Sorry, grandfather." Tom felt his face flame. "I wouldn't miss walking across the stage and getting my college scholarship for anything."

"It has been taken care of. Young Eagle will get the paper later."

Tom gritted his teeth and clenched his hands. "I wish you'd call me Tom and I'm not going."

"I have spoken." Walking Eagle dismissed his great-grandson's arguments and marched out, every bit the grand chief he had once been.

Tom dropped into a chair. "Why can't he wait until after graduation if we have to take this stupid trip? It's only a few weeks away." He shuddered. He loved Grandfather but the last thing he needed was to head into the woods with a man so old he might keel over any minute.

Notice that I didn't change plot, characters or setting. Instead, I:
- **dumped passive** *was* and over-use of exclamation mark
- **added color** to characters/conflict with word pictures
- **showed** Tom's anger and Walking Eagle's refusal to listen instead of merely *telling* about them.

These simple changes add depth and feeling to the key opening scene.

DEBUGGING THE DRAFT

A good way to discover "brands of beginners" is to highlight them.
You may be shocked at how many you find. (I was when I did this.)

1. A single snowflake is lovely. A multitude creates havoc. So do **small words that infest our writing.**

that—Write: I knew he was coming, not I knew that he was coming.

said—"I am going to town," Mary *said,* running to her room is better written as, "I am going to town." Mary ran to her room.
   Often writers try so hard to avoid said their stories sound like some of the original Nancy Drew stories. Nancy and her friends seldom said anything. They "retorted indignantly," "exclaimed delightedly," etc. Other authors have characters "quip," "sibilate," etc. **Note:** Never have your characters "laugh" or "smile" their words. Words can be "spoken, cried, hissed," etc. but *not* "laughed, smiled," and so on. "I can't help it," Pete smiled is incorrect. Use: "I can't help it." Pete smiled.

would—Rather than, Joe's father would take him on his lap and would tell him stories, say, Joe's father took him on his lap and told him stories.

was/were/is/are—Writers' most-often repeated word. Use action and character movement most of the time. Caroline was standing at the door, frantically pounding for admittance becomes Caroline frantically pounded on the door. "Let me in!"
   Dull description: The grass was green. The daffodils were yellow. **Word pictures:** Lemon-yellow daffodils dotted the emerald grass like chunks of living sunlight.

had—Use once or twice to get into the far past then switch to simple past tense so readers can feel they are there. Tom *had* watched his father bridle the horse a hundred times. Dad *had* welcomed his help even though his fingers *had* been awkward and young—puts distance between reader/characters. **Try:** Tom had watched his father bridle the horse a hundred times. Dad welcomed the help, even though Tom's awkward young fingers often fumbled.

DEBUGGING THE DRAFT, page 2

Very— Contrary to popular opinion, the word very weakens rather than strengthening. *She is lovely* speaks for itself. *She is very lovely* sounds fawning and contrived.

Just, only—can be insulting. "*Just* a housewife, *only* a janitor." Avoid it.

Because—A real tell-tale word. Never write: 'The reason Parker did (whatever) is *because*...." Readers are jerked from story and think, "Oh yeah, the author's right in there explaining the story." Let your characters and story **show** why Parker chose this action.

Of course, in fact—Again—editorializing by the author, besides being over-used.

"ing" and "ly" words—Use sparingly. "The fire raged" is far more active and interesting than "The fire burned hotly."

As—First runner-up to "was" as the biggest pest word, it creeps in and multiplies faster than a new calculator. "Terry smiled *as* Lori turned toward him" is fine—until as is used again and again. (I once found a dozen plus *as* uses in three pages of a good writer's work!) Ways to eliminate *as*: (1) a period: "Lori turned toward him. Terry smiled." (2) the word *and*: "Lori turned toward him and Terry smiled." (3) the word *when* (but don't get too many of those, either): "*When* Lori turned toward him, Terry smiled."

Seemed to, almost, nearly—These are "weasel words," sneaky ones that weaken by qualifying. "The smoke *almost/seemed to/nearly* choked him." Either the smoke choked him or it didn't. Say so. **Exception:** When viewpoint character is speaking of something only another character can know, it **must** be qualified. "It *seemed* to Travis, Melissa no longer cared whether he called."

But, And, Well, Then, For—Don't use to start sentences, except in rare cases for emphasis. I ended **Delayed Dream**, sequel to YA novel **Interrupted Flight** (2-in-one book) with a diary entry that shows Andrea's growth and looks ahead (see next page).

DEBUGGING THE DRAFT, page 3

"The Andrea I am now doesn't have to delay her dream. Next fall Dori and I will start college and nurses' training. And just maybe the exciting future ..."

2. **Changing verb tense.** <u>Wrong</u>: Jody *crosses* the bridge and *walked* to the farm. <u>Right</u>: Either, Jody crosses the bridge and walks to the farm or Jody crossed the bridge and walked to the farm.

3. **Changing viewpoint.** Remember, **stay inside your lead character** and present what she sees/hears/suspects/thinks. Stay outside all others, except for facial expressions, movements, dialogue, etc. With few exceptions, short stories should be from *one* character's viewpoint, spotlighting him at all times. Novels can have more than one viewpoint but focus should change between major scenes or chapters.

4. **Sentence/paragraph length.** Keep short and crisp to build tension, conflict or suspense. A bit longer gives a softer mood. Examples: Rain slammed the roof like bullets. It finally dwindled to trickles and an apologetic sun peered from behind a cloud.

5. **Short phrases,** like these, set off by commas, make run-on sentences.

6. **Over-explaining.** Don't. Hit point once. Hard. Go on.

7. **Pet phrases or words.** "A sulky sun" is effective once, boring the next time. Avoid repeating the same descriptive word(s) in too close proximity. Don't repeat pet phrases. <u>Familiarity breeds contempt</u>.

8. **Clichés** (too-common phrases), **buzz words, incorrect usage.** Create your own word images or do takeoffs on clichés. A clever title changed 'every nook and cranny' to "Every Crook and Nanny." Currently used are *"scenario"* and *"this point in time"* (redundant). <u>Double check word meanings</u>. *"Nauseous"* means disgusting; *"nauseated"* refers to sickness.

9. **Modern sounding words.** Many long term words can sound too modern because of current over-use. Avoid using in historicals.

10. **Commas, Exclamation marks.** Cut drastically.

DEBUGGING THE DRAFT, page 4

11. **Paragraphing dialogue.** Keep speaker's words and actions in the same paragraph (even though some books don't do this) and change to a new paragraph with each speaker/actor. **Example:**
    "Honey, have you seen my keys?" Joe stamped into the room.
    "I don't have them."
    He raised one eyebrow. "Did I say you did?" A look of patient resignation crossed his rugged face. "Why can't you—"
    "Forget it." Alice stormed out before he could criticize her again.

12. **Names and places.** Name people, places, things. Add interest by being specific. Rather than, "A car arrived," say: "A bright red Ford Escort pulled into the driveway." **Exception:** Characters who have little significance to the story should remain the pharmacist, clerk, etc.

13. **No quotation marks around thoughts**; it confuses them with dialogue.

14. **Spelling and grammar.** Check, recheck, double check. A small spelling dictionary on your desk is an absolute must.

15. **Intersperse characters' names** with he/she, him/her for variety.

16. In two-character conversation **do not have characters continually refer to one another by name.** The story should show who is speaking.

17. **Don't write in dialect**; it's too hard to read. Instead, choose colloquialisms and expressions that give a feel of place and time. Or give an individual character a habit/expression that shows setting.

18. **Avoid slang** that will be out of date before your article/story/book is printed. Choose timeless descriptions to convey the message (especially important in children's and young adult books).

19. **Read your manuscript aloud.** This is the single best way to catch word and phrase repetition, stilted dialogue.

20. Remember—**dialogue is not conversation, but the essence of it.** You don't repeat a whole conversation, just the gist of what is said.

REJECTION-PROOFING TIPS

Before you submit your final version of any manuscript, you need to
     evaluate content/style, etc. to ensure your work is as salable as possible.
Every story/book/article should pass the following test of high standards,
     though *not all* tips apply to every manuscript.

1. Grab readers in the beginning.
2. Hang onto them in the middle.
3. Satisfy with an acceptable ending.
4. Don't have so many characters they detract from "star(s)."
5. Clearly establish the <u>overall</u> mood (many moods may be included).
6. Be sure plot and setting are believable.
7. Document facts. Give credit where necessary.
8. Watch for too many or too long flashbacks. Avoid foreshadowing.
9. Don't let minor characters steal the spotlight for too long.
10. Choose character with most to lose or win for the lead.
11. <u>Show what happens, don't tell</u>--especially after the fact. Readers don't want to hear about an earthquake but to see and feel it.
12. Intersperse dialogue/description/narration.
13. Keep characters "in character."
14. If there's to be a drastic change in a character, plant clues.
15. Stick with your theme.
16. Don't interrupt active scenes with meditation like, *"If I live through hanging from this cliff I'll always remember the flowers,"* etc.
17. Don't be cutesy; avoid the trite and meaningless.
18. Play fair with readers by weaving in clues to mysteries.
19. Avoid beginning, "If I had known then what I know now." This shows reader that no matter what happens, storyteller survives.
20. Use a fresh slant/new information when writing the familiar.
21. Know what you're writing: setting, subject matter, facts.
22. Be sure manuscript is logical.
23. Lead character must solve his or her own problem.
24. End in the right place, the natural closing--and not too abruptly.
25. Be honest: is manuscript precious only to you?
26. Avoid being too autobiographical. You lose objectivity.
27. Something really worthwhile must happen.
28. Brief, vivid description lets readers fill in some of the blanks. Don't over-explain and take this joy from those who buy your work.

REJECTION PROOFING TIPS, page 2

29. Cut every word that doesn't move story/article/book forward.
30. Secure written permission to quote anything that might be questioned.
31. Get your manuscript "back to the beginning" or title at the end when it will add to your story/book/article.
32. Search for a "quirk" that can set your manuscript apart.
33. Ask yourself, *Is this the best work I can do at this time, or will further research, revision, etc. improve it?* (If you feel it can be improved, list why you feel that way and what you will do to make it better.)_____

_____

_____

_____

Finally:

a. If you had not written the story or article, would you buy the magazine in order to read it completely after scanning the first two paragraphs? Why or why not?_____

_____

_____

_____

_____

b. If you had not written the book, would you buy a copy after reading no more than the first two pages? The Table of Contents and first two pages of a nonfiction book? Why or why not?

_____

_____

_____

_____

_____

Congratulations! Your manuscript is ready for the last test.

FINAL CHECKLIST

____1. Is address correct? Do you have correct postage? SASE or postcard?

____2. Is query, proposal or manuscript addressed to an editor <u>by name?</u>

____3. Have you researched to be sure the company does this type work?

____4. Is your submission professional: double-spaced, except for query; wide margins; clear, dark print (no obviously dot matrix, all caps, script type, etc.); invisible corrections; no typos/spelling errors.

____5. If you can furnish disk, have you told editor? Include computer or word processing information such as <u>IBM, Word for Windows, 6.0.</u>

____6. Approximate length given? Available photos described?

____7. Cover letter for books or notation for magazines as to whether it's an article or short story?

____8. Are you really qualified to write a book/article on this subject? Why?

____9. Did you check your library's Periodical Index or *BOOKS IN PRINT* and mention competition, plus how your work differs?

____10. Are you willing to revise as requested?

____11. Is your work free from prejudice, condemnation, preaching?

____12. If written in first person, have you kept the number of "I" uses down?

____13. Is it well-written, fast-paced, interesting, timely?

____14. Have you refrained from copying another's style and used your own? *Never try to write like your favorite author.*

____15. Have you discovered/observed company's taboos?

If you have even one "no" answer, you aren't ready to submit. Make the necessary corrections then send off your manuscript. Good luck!

PART 9: Perseverance Pays

You've come a long way, from idea to complete, submitted manuscript. Now you face the waiting game, a possible acceptance or return (rejection). **The best way to beat anxiety is to begin another manuscript.**

Keep on studying the market, making your best even better. Most of all: **Don't let turn-downs get you down!** They're simply part of the job.

Editors send manuscripts back for many reasons, including:
⇒ they have just assigned, run or purchased something too similar
⇒ magazine is changing slant or buying less unsolicited material
⇒ the editor read it before he had his morning coffee

The important thing is to keep your manuscripts in the mail until sold. The manuscript that never sells is the one in your desk drawer. If it comes back, so what? You're in good company. It's often said:

LOUIS L'AMOUR received 200 rejections before selling anything.
JANE YOLEN (children's author) had 113 returns her first year freelancing but kept going because of a scrawled note on the bottom of one rejection slip, "Try us again."
DR. SEUSS had 23 publishers reject *And To Think I Saw it on Mulberry Street*.
ZANE GREY wept against a lamp post after being told, "You can neither write fiction nor nonfiction. Try another line of work." The same company later sold millions of copies of his books.

Some of my books sell on the first try. **Some take years**, because the subject or style aren't right for the market at that time.

Example: In the summer of 1994 I received a go-ahead from a new proposal to revise my biblical novel *BELATED FOLLOWER*. I had collected 32 rejections and spent a bundle in postage submitting it for the past 17 years. **What if I had given up on the 10th try?** The 27th?

Even worse, what if after the 32nd homing-pigeon-act I'd stopped believing in my book and told myself, "It will never sell." Heartsong Presents hadn't done biblical novels. However, my editor liked my style and the story. He plans to publish it in the winter, 1995-96.

MULTIPLE SALES

If you are the rare author who sells all your manuscripts to prestigious magazines such as *Reader's Digest, Guideposts, Good Housekeeping*, etc. skip this section.

If you're like most of us, you'll need to **"pay your dues"** by accumulating credits (sales). Writing for smaller magazines, especially if you're working in the inspirational field, offers a chance to be read, earn some money and learn along the way.

Many small magazines offset their lower payment to writers by purchasing one time/simultaneous or reprint rights. (Review PART 3, RIGHTS.) This means the acceptance or publication of your story or article is just the beginning. **Two rules govern multiple sales: (1) You must submit only to companies that accept simultaneous, one time or reprint rights, and (2) You must offer to magazines whose readerships do not compete.**

Example: Presbyterians, Pentecostals, Catholics, etc. all read different magazines. If you have a general interest inspirational manuscript, several denominations may be interested. On the other hand, if you write a family-oriented story that interests many ages, you mustn't send it to both a Baptist adult magazine and a Baptist teen or children's Sunday School paper and so on. They will probably end up in the same home and be in competition with one another.

Getting more mileage out of manuscripts is the only real gravy train I'm aware exists. Reason—the hard work of writing has already been done. The price of a stamp is all that's required. Whatever you make on resales has cost you far less than your original investment of time and energy.

Original material sometimes sells simultaneously. However, I do far better reselling stories and articles after they've been printed.

Example: In **1992** (in addition to books) I sold 22 articles; 10 were reprints and only two were simultaneous sales. In **1993** I sold a whopping 55 stories. Only 21 were originals, the others were all reprints.

> **Interesting note: Many times I've received two or three times as much money for a reprint sale than it brought in the first time around.**

USING THE **H-A-S** METHOD

I separate markets for "multi-purpose manuscripts" into three categories:

<u>H</u>omonym   <u>A</u>ntonym   <u>S</u>ynonym

Homonym markets are those that use similar material but focus on different audience, such as various ages. **Example:** A mysterious experience in my father's family when he was a boy became **"Stranger at the Door."** It has sold 21 times to Christian magazines ranging from children's through senior adult's, reached millions with its heartwarming message and brought in about $1000 since first accepted in 1981. It also appeared in the premiere edition of *Angels on Earth,* a Guideposts publication.

Antonym markets have little or nothing in common, i.e., secular as opposed to religious markets. **"Six Days Make One Weak"** is a tongue-in-cheek, nostalgic comparison of my great-grandparents' life and work in the early 1900's with present-day living. It sold to two rural magazines, *IDEALS*, one Christian magazine and was reprinted in an anthology. **"My Store-Boughten Christmas"** delighted primaries through senior adults in 13 Christian and secular magazines before appearing in a devotional book. Its universal appeal made it a good candidate for multiple sales. (See pgs 90-91.)

Synonym markets consistently use the same kind of material. My short story about a courageous teen who refuses to drink with his teammates, **"And the Winner is..."** sold to 10 magazines with its message of encouragement to those struggling to be accepted without giving in to peer pressure. More than a million copies of Christian adult magazines have carried, **"White Water and Quiet Streams,"** an article on marriage. They represent many denominations, all concerned with helping families form strong ties and stay together.

Out of print books can occasionally be resold. My early teen book, ***THE SUMMER OF PETER AND PAM*** (Baker Books) was reissued by Review and Herald as ***SANDWICH ISLAND SUMMER***. Barbour Books reprinted three out of print historicals after rights reverted to me.

MY STORE-BOUGHTEN CHRISTMAS

Every Christmas of my life has been special. Our family looks forward to celebrating Christ's birth with our own family traditions. Although some of them have changed over the years, many remain the same—the decorating, the joy, the delight in preparing surprises for all.

Yet of all the Christmases I have had, one stands out in my memory. There I learned the meaning of giving on my first "store-boughten" Christmas so long ago.

I was born in 1935, a time scarce in money, abundant in love. We had plenty to eat and wear, a good warm home but very little cash.

Each Christmas all the relatives gathered at Grandma's. Somehow the womenfolk had found time and enough money to provide gifts for every family member--and it usually meant 30 gifts! Fancy embroidered towels, pillowcases, kitchen utensils for the women; warm socks, books for the men. It required planning from one year to the next, checking and rechecking so no one was left out.

Wrappings offered another challenge. Even today it hurts me to see careless fingers eagerly tear into beautiful paper. We saved and ironed every scrap, every inch of reusable ribbon, or did without.

At eight or nine, things changed. I wouldn't be making gifts for my family that year. My gifts would be "store-boughten!" Never was a little girl more thrilled than when we started out early one December Saturday morning on our annual Christmas shopping trip. Fifty miles from our small home town in the Washington Cascade Mountains lay Everett, the "big town." It looked like fairyland on our infrequent visits. All those stores, huge buildings, elevators. Wonderful!

Yet even they had lost their charm. My gaze fastened on only one area. Three large ten-cent stores: Woolworth, Kresses and Newberry, all in the same block, offered hours of shopping adventure. My two brothers and I were perfectly safe there and could wander while Dad and Mom took care of buying all the other gifts.

My sweaty hand inside my mitten clutched a vast fortune, the means to purchase my four gifts. An entire dollar, one hundred pennies magically turned into four shining silver quarters. Never had anyone felt so rich.

We all had chores at home. The boys carried wood and pumped water. I helped in the house. But when we wanted to earn money we turned to what we called "the windows-and-cupboards." Five cents for washing a large section of windows. Ten cents for the cupboards. My wealth represented weeks of shining clean windows-and-cupboards. Not for anything would I spend it on myself. Happiness that I could buy gifts for Mom, Dad and the boys warmed me.

Mom's gift was easy, the first year I saw artificial Christmas corsages. Holly, ribbon, a tiny cone glitter-sprinkled like snow. It cost exactly $.25, the amount I knew I could spend. Four quarters, four gifts meant $.25 apiece.

I can't remember my older brother's present, but it also cost a quarter. Pride and wonder filled me. How well my shopping was going. I'd just been through the stores once and after only two hours I was half done.

Then I hit a snag. I saw on a high counter what I wanted for my little brother. A metal bank, but what a bank! The clerk dropped a coin into it. The little monkey with blue pants, red jacket and friendly smile tipped his hat! I held my breath and asked, "How much is it?"

I can't remember a more bitter disappointment than when the clerk told me it cost $.29, four pennies more than I dared spend. Otherwise, I'd only have $.21 for Dad's gift. I turned away, never thinking to find and ask my folks for extra money. We'd been taught to solve our own problems. Why had I even seen the little monkey bank when I couldn't afford it?

Who is to say the Author of Christmas doesn't recognize childish disappointments? I don't call it a miracle yet was it a little more than

chance? As I walked the narrow aisles, I saw a display of bandannas like those Dad used as hankies in his woods work. *They were $.21!* I quickly bought a blue one and raced away. *What if the monkey bank had been sold?*

It hadn't. It smiled just as warmly while I counted out my last quarter and four pennies.

My family loved their "store-boughten gifts," especially Randy. He put in pennies, laughed, then shook them out and put them in again. I had spent $1.00 and gained $1000 happiness.

Years have gone. The family circle is smaller. Yet every time I see a snowflake or go shopping, I look back to my "store-boughten" Christmas. I don't remember my gifts that year. The joyous surprise on my family's faces was enough.

Perhaps that's why I've never felt Christmas was too commercialized. I love the preparations, ringing bells, special church services and using what I have as best I can.

Long ago the Wise Men came, bringing gifts. On my first "store-boughten" Christmas I knew how they felt--and still do.

FACING THE DRAGON

> One of my favorite illustrations is the story of a small boy who refused to open his closet door. He insisted a dragon lived inside.
>
> His wise mother didn't laugh. She gently took his hand and said, "We must face the dragon. We'll find out if he's friendly or cross and why he lives in the closet."
>
> The dragon turned out to be a trick of light that reflected and distorted the child's image when he opened the closet door. This in no way destroyed the little boy's thrill of pride. He and his mother had not only faced but vanquished the dragon.

The story-dragon and little boy are the same. The name of every writer's dragon is **self-doubt**. He must be faced and vanquished. With every return, self-doubt rears his ugly head, smirks and roars, "See? I knew you couldn't do it." **Don't listen or feel guilty** when he gets in your face and accuses you of not writing as much as you want to and feel you should.

Respond to these "facing the dragon" questions.
Be honest and realistic:

Answer on separate paper so you can go back every six months or so, "face the dragon" again and reevaluate your writing maturity and growth.

⇒ How many times will I send a manuscript out? Why?

⇒ Am I able to accept an editor's criticism? Why? To what extent?

⇒ Is my writing as good as I can make it **at this time**? If so, why do I deserve to be published? If not, how can I improve?

⇒ How much time this week will I sacrifice to write?

⇒ What will I give up in order to write? (Mowing the lawn and cleaning the bathrooms are not acceptable answers.)

⇒ What is a realistic daily or weekly goal (amount of time) for my writing?

⇒ Do I want to write or just to "be a writer?" Why?

⇒ Am I willing to view writing as a profession and study accordingly?

FACING THE DRAGON, page 2

⇒ What are my short range goals--6 months to a year?
What are my long range goals? Where would I like to be 5 years
from now? 10? 20? What, if anything, is stopping me? Is it temporary
(such as lack of time due to small children) or permanent (fear, etc.)?

⇒ Am I secure enough to handle rejection or will it tear me down and make
me question my self-worth because of pressure/stress in other life areas?
*This question is vitally important. Even calling rejections "returns"
cannot completely take away a sense of disappointment or failure.*

More Facing the Dragon: Weigh the Choices, Beat the Blues

You can't control editorial decisions but you do have choices in various
situations. Considering your response ahead of time can be valuable.

1. **When someone doesn't like your manuscript:**
   —throw away your typewriter/sell your computer [Forget it]
   —consider his/her credentials/qualifications to judge
   —recognize this is *one person's opinion,* nothing more
   —determine to work harder

2. **When you receive five rejections in a row on your novel/story/article:**
   —tear it up, delete it from the computer, bury it [Wrong]
   —keep sending it out as long as editors will request it
   —review in the light of current market trends; revise if necessary
   —feel editors have little or bad taste [OK to feel it, just don't say it.]

3. **When a great idea you proposed earned a turn down from a leading
   magazine, yet appears under someone else's by-line a month later:**
   —don't believe an editor stole and reassigned it [Untrue in 99.9% of cases]
   —do recognize that others can have the same unique ideas you do
   —do allow for the time lag between acceptance and printing
   —don't write the magazine off as crooked

FACING THE DRAGON, page 3

4. When an editor writes "try us again" on a rejection:
—don't feel it's a way of being nice [Editors can't take time]
—don't view it as an open door for anything you write
—take it for exactly that, an invitation to try **suitable** material again

Send another manuscript with a brief note reminding editor he liked the earlier one enough to jot a note. **Example:** Dear Mr. Webster, Although you were unable to use my recent submission, "Help, the Sky is Falling," I appreciated your invitation to try again. Perhaps you will enjoy the enclosed "Four Ways to Tame Your Toddler." Thank you for your response.

5. If you are asked to rewrite a manuscript:
—don't send it elsewhere [You may miss out on a sale.]
—do, unless it compromises your principles or destroys your manuscript
—show the editor you are dependable by following her suggestions
—don't feel the work is perfect as written and refuse [Reconsider]

6. When a magazine that has bought from you rejects a new piece:
—feel they are no longer interested in you as an author [False]
—they may be overstocked or have recently bought something similar
—their needs may have changed
—they may have a new editor

7. Following item # 6 you should:
—write and ask why [Not if you want the editor to accept future work.]
—send something else that matches their stated needs
—request new guidelines if they are available [Be sure to send SASE.]
—recognize even the friendliest editors can't like or use *all* your work

8. When a publisher holds your manuscript far too long:
—demand a response immediately [You'll get it—but won't like it.]
—send a low key follow-up [Example: Part 1, page 3]

If you don't get an answer in a reasonable length of time, send a second letter stating you are withdrawing the manuscript from their consideration. (Alternative: State you are no longer offering exclusive rights to consider [book] or First Serial rights [magazine] and will be sending to other publishers/magazines in view of company's delayed response.)

APPENDIX

HOW LONG IS A ...

KIND OF MANUSCRIPT	APPROXIMATE WORDS
Short-short story	500-2500
Short story	2500-4000
Novelette	7000-15,000
Novel, Adult	45,000-150,000+
Children's picture book	500-1000+
Juvenile/Young adult book	15,000-75,000+
Nonfiction book	Depends on subject
Poem	2-100+ lines (many magazines like 4-16)
Query letter	1 single spaced page

Reminder: When proposing a book/story/article, give planned word length.

> ## *Always* check magazine and book publisher's market lists and guidelines for their specific word lengths.

RÉSUMÉ, sample

Colleen L. Reece, **Full time author/teacher/speaker since 1978**
Voted Favorite Author, 1993 & 1994, Heartsong Presents Book Club

General Information

Writing instructor: Green River Community College; Auburn WA Senior. Center

Former Writer's Digest School correspondence instructor and *Writer's Digest*
  magazine correspondent

Guest speaker at schools, conferences, church, civic and writing groups

26 years secretarial/administrative assistant in Washington State schools, Veterans
  and Bonneville Power Administrations.

20+ years camp counseling, elementary through young adult

Church and Bible school teacher, elementary through senior adult

Born and raised in Darrington, Washington, setting for many books

---

Writing credits

93 books accepted or published to date, including:

- picture book text; children's books—adventure, devotional, serials
- teen/YA novels—Christian, secular, high interest/low read. level
- adventure, mystery, pioneer/western,* romance, family values novels (both fictional
  and based on true events); historical and contemporary
- foreign rights sales to: Australia, Brazil, Denmark, England, Finland, Indonesia,
  Italy, Sweden

1200+ article/short story/children's story sales, including:

- business articles/pamphlets: *National Research Bureau*
- how-to writing articles: *Writer's Digest, Pen Woman*
- nostalgia/humor: *Mature Living, Ideals*
- Christian leadership: *Youth Leader, Cornerstone Connections, Advance*
- inspirational and Christian stories/articles to a wide variety of magazines ranging
  from *Guide* to *Guideposts, R-A-D-A-R* to *Reader's Digest*

BOOK LIST, sample

Presenting: BOOKS YOU CAN TRUST by Colleen L. Reece. All family oriented.

These are the most available of my 93 accepted or published books. Many early titles are out of print. Some can still be found in libraries and occasionally, in used book stores.

Barbour Books
Romance Reader flip books
Honor Bound/The Calling of Elizabeth Courtland
To Love and Cherish/Storm Clouds over Chantel
Legacy of Silver/Angel of the North
The Hills of Hope/A Girl Called Cricket
Present Tense (YA) flip book:

Interrupted Flight/Delayed Dream +
Western Collection flip book: *
Voices in the Desert/Echoes in the Valley +

Heartsong Presents
A Torch for Trinity
Candleshine +
Wildflower Harvest
Desert Rose +
Veiled Joy
Tapestry of Tamar +
Crows'-Nests and Mirrors
(with Albert B. Towne)

Western Trails Quartet *
Silence in the Sage
Whispers in the Wilderness +
Music in the Mountains +
Captives of the Canyon +

- sequel; * Gary Dale, pseudonym
** Connie Loraine, pseudonym

New contemporary Shepherd of Love Hospital Series **
Book 1: Lamp in Darkness
Book 2: Flickering Flames +
Book 3: A Kindled Spark   +

New Historical Flower Chronicles
Book 1: Flower of Seattle
Book 2: Flower of the West +
Book 3: Flower of the North +
Book 4: Flower of Alaska   +

Young Reader's Christian Library and Barbour Books
Prudence of Plymouth Plantation
Pollyanna, condensed and retold
Pollyanna Grows Up, cond./retold +
Heidi, condensed/retold
Pollyanna Plays the Game (new)
Pollyanna Comes Home + (new
Little Women, condensed and retold

Review and Herald (youth)
For the Love of Mike
JUMPSTART! (Jr. devotional)
Mysterious Treadle Machine
P.K. the Great
Plain, Plain Melissa Jane
Sandwich Island Summer

Kaleidoscope Press
WRITING SMARTER, not harder,
The Workbook Way

LETTERHEAD, Sample

COLLEEN L. REECE
Author/Teacher/Speaker
Street address
City, state and zip code
Area code/phone

Books You Can Trust

TIPS:

Don't say William Johnson, Writer (anyone who writes is a writer)

Okay to use Allan Davis, Author (this shows you're published)

⇒ If you want a logo and/or motto, keep it simple. Don't give every title you possess. I've seen letterhead so over-loaded with author accomplishments the clutter left little space to write. Save the credentials for your résumé.

Have it printed on quality, non-erasable white bond, at least 20 lb.

⇒ Don't skimp by using photocopy paper. Your first impression is important.

⇒ Buying envelopes in quantity (minimum 500) through the U.S. Stamped Envelope Agency (get form at Post Office) brings money savings plus they imprint your name, title and return address free.

SALES RECORD, Year_____   ✔ **= posted to account book**

DATE	TITLE/ ITEM	SOLD TO	RIGHTS and # WORDS	PAY	TOTAL

SUBMISSIONS RECORD

TITLE_____ ITEM_____ WORDS_____

SENT TO:	DATE:	Pays on Acceptance Publication	Reporting time, Rights purchased
1.			
2.			
3.			
4.			
5.			
6.			
7.			
8.			
9.			
10.			
11.			
12.			
13.			
14.			

BACKUP MARKETS:	

QUICK REFERENCE CHART ©1991 by Colleen L. Reece, Sample

Novel Title _____ Date/place _____

CHARACTERS: Names/nicknames special meaning, relationship, age_	Height/ Weight	Hair/ Eyes	Birthdate/ Birthplace	Other significant notes
ANDREW (Andy) CULLEN *means strong, manly.* 19 at beginning of CAPTIVES OF THE CANYON	5' 9" 160 lbs. muscular	ripe corn, shocky/ sparkly brown	1-5-1873/ Tonto Basin, Arizona	Says doggone and ain't. Wide cheerful grin. Rides chestnut mare Chinquapin (Chinq). Chases black stallion Sheik.

OTHER IMPORTANT INFO., i.e., home/setting/town/area/animals, etc.

Example: "The Contraption" -- 2-seated/high-wheeled buggy drawn by matched bays; David (right) and Goliath.

ACKNOWLEDGMENTS

Some of **THE WORKBOOK WAY** charts, etc. are based on material that originally appeared in various magazines. For example, the 7-page character chart grew from my 36 question chart featured in the popular article, "Just a Bunch of Words: How to Develop Believable Characters" *(Writer's Digest*, 1981). Actual excerpts have been credited when used.

Canadian Author and Bookman
 1981
"More Defensive Measures"
"Quality? No Question"
"Rx for Writers"

The Christian Writer
"Better Scene than Heard," 1986
"Happily Ever After," 1984

Christian Writers' Newsletter
"How to Write Quality Queries,"
   1982

"Who Gets the Manuscript?" 1983

Freelance Writer's Report, 1982
"Getting Started"
"Selling Your Fiction"

The Inkling, 1985

"Chart Your Article's Course"

WDS Forum
"Beginners Mistakes in Short Story
   Writing," 1980

"It Pays to Plot," 1981

"Know Your Characters," 1980

"3 Beginner's Blocks to Sales,"
   1982

Writer's Digest
"Ankle Deep in Warm Tears:

 How to Make Nostalgia Pay,"
 1980
 "Eight Ways to Make Editors
   Smile," 1983

"Job Work," 1983
"Just a Bunch of Words," 1981
"Keeping Your Short Stories
 Short," 1987
"Quick Reference Chart,"
   (purchased 1991)

"Only the Unqualified need Apply,"
   1984

"Simon Retorts...Exclaims...States...
 Simon Says," 1984
"Tell-Tale Signs," 1985
"Writing a Bike," 1983

The Writer's Nook News
"Multi-Purpose Manuscripts make
 Money," 1994

"Blind Date," originally published by **Listen** Magazine, February 1988

"Tips for Trips with Older Travelers," **Vibrant Life**, July/August, 1992

"My Store Boughten Christmas," **The Ruralite**,* December 1978 (**not a*

good market for nostalgia—my story sale was an exception.)

"Pre-write," don't rewrite with:

blank outline forms & charts

Created and used for 20 years, resulting in
93 books and over 1200 story & article sales.

$4.95

SmartSheets are from
Colleen L. Reece's
Writing Smarter, not harder, The Workbook Way

Kaleidoscope Press **2507 94th Ave. E., Puyallup, WA 98371**
(206) 848-1116   Order Toll-Free 1-800-977-READ [code] MORE

Special offer!—30% off 10 pads or more of one title

Send _____ *SmartSheets* pads (96-100 pgs) **at *$4.95 ea.** (postage paid) (.25 tax in WA)

_____ **S.Stories, 50 2-pg outlines**   _____ **Characters, 16 6-page outlines**
_____ **Book, 25 2-pg novel, 25 NF, 25 ch. outlines** _____ **Articles, 50 2-pg outlines**

□**Check** □**VISA** □**Mastercard** □**30% off 10 pads of 1 title**

Card #_____ **Expir.** _____ **Phone**_____

Print name_____ **Sign**_____

City/State/Zip_____

(Photocopies of this order form are permitted, or write to the publisher)

Who needs this writing workbook?

"I do!" say award-winning full-time author Colleen L. Reece
(93 published/accepted books & over 1200 story/article sales in the past 20 years).

You do too, if you've ever said...

"I need to learn the basics?"
"How can I find the time to write?"
"Show me how to write for today's markets."
"My ideas and endings are good, but my middles fall apart."
"How can I write faster, yet retain quality?"
"I want o write well enough to get paid for it."
"Help me choose creative, fresh ideas."
"Light a motivational fire under me!"

$13.95

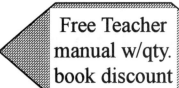

Free Teacher manual w/qty. book discount

Writing Smarter, not harder, The Workbook Way:

⇒ helps you prepare, with step-by-step suggestions, *before* you start writing,
⇒ contains 112 pages of informal, easy, straightforward & effective helps
⇒ increases your output /sales through "pre-writing," & less rewriting
⇒ gives you a solid background for starting & completing your manuscript
⇒ is portable; can be used anywhere, in short spaces of time
⇒ includes thought-provoking questions, with completed & blank worksheets

Kaleidoscope Press **2507 94th Ave. E., Puyallup, WA 98371**

(206) 848-1116 Order Toll-Free 1-800-977-READ [code] MORE

Special offers!—Free Teacher's Manual ($5) & 30% off 10 book minimum

---

Send_____ copies of *Writing Smarter*...at $13.95 & $1.50 ship ea. (1.15 tax, WA)

☐Check ☐VISA ☐Mastercard ☐Pur. Order ☐Free Teacher's Manual
(10 book minimum, & 30% discount)

Card #_____Expiration_____Phone_____

Print name_____Signature_____

City/State/Zip_____

(Photocopies of this page are permitted, or write to above address)